The Best ot
Ogonyok

Ogonyok is probably the most important and influential magazine in the world today. Founded in 1923 in Moscow, it has become a flagship of glasnost under its radical new editor, Vitaly Korotich.

Its mixture of bold reportage and challenging exploration of the country's cruel history has trebled sales to more than three million. According to Rupert Cornwell of the *Independent*, 'it is the most outspoken press defender of liberalism and reform in the land'. But by criticising powerful politicians and exposing high-level corruption, it has earned the wrath of officialdom and in a recent letter to *Pravda* it was described as the 'scum bubbling on the crust of the mighty stream of renewal'. There have been numerous attempts to isolate the magazine and curb its circulation; one of its young journalists was killed while investigating organised crime, and Korotich is now a national celebrity, loved or loathed with an intensity that intellectuals excite only in Russia.

This selection of the best of *Ogonyok* during the last two years offers the reader a ride on the most exciting rollercoaster in the world today, the rollercoaster of glasnost. From Moscow gang-warfare to bribery and corruption, Stalin's war crimes to the rehabilitation of leading intellectuals, the Armenian earthquake to Afghanistan, ethnic unrest in Azerbaijan to the rising suicide rate, shortages in the shops to the drug trade, here is a fascinating collection of articles which for the first time provides a vivid, first-hand view of what it is like to live in the Soviet Union during this period of dramatic change.

The Best of *Ogonyok*
The New Journalism of Glasnost

Edited by
VITALY
KOROTICH

Edited and
translated by
CATHY
PORTER

HEINEMANN
LONDON

William Heinemann Ltd
Michelin House, 81 Fulham Road, London SW3 6RB
LONDON   MELBOURNE   AUCKLAND

First published 1990
Selection copyright © 1990 V. Korotich,
Ogonyok Magazine, 14 Bumazhny proezd, Moscow, USSR
Translation copyright © 1990 Cathy Porter

A CIP catalogue record for this book
is available from the British Library
ISBN 0 434 59586 1

Photoset by Rowland Phototypesetting Ltd
Bury St Edmunds, Suffolk
Printed and bound in Great Britain
by BPCC Hazell Books Ltd, Aylesbury, Bucks.

Contents

Foreword
Vitaly Korotich

It seems to me that the reason *Ogonyok* has been able to publish the articles in this book is not that we are a talented people, but that our people have discovered their dignity. That, I think, is the most important thing now. Solving our economic problems will be a long, slow process, but the fresh air of glasnost blowing through the windows has changed us irrevocably. We may not yet be as well fed as we would wish, but we are far more honest, more courageous, more accessible to the rest of humanity, and a more reliable part of it.

Rejoice with us that events have moved so rapidly, for what is happening provides us with a powerful argument in support of our indestructible humanism. Remember, we used to be told that it was right to follow orders that were alien to us and to denounce our friends, that the only beautiful church was a demolished church, that democratic elections were impossible . . . We were told all this and much more, yet how quickly we have unlearned these lessons in brutality! The articles here, then, may be read as monologues of people learning to speak again after a long silence, and realising that the right to truth is equal to the right to life, and that in some circumstances this right may take precedence over all else. This is so now.

In our country there used to be banned subjects, forbidden names, and authors whom it was impossible to publish. Now that we are throwing off the gag of officialdom, the country is becoming closer to its citizens, and citizens are demanding more of their country. We are no longer afraid. We have not yet learnt to sing hymns to equality, but we have found our voice. Many of the articles in this book were written by people who were brought up on lies, but who have refused to accept these lies as the basis for their lives. We do not publish professional liars. And you must not publish them either. Eradicating falsehood is a universal task; if the power of the lie diminishes in our country or in yours, it diminishes throughout humanity as a whole.

The magazine which has published these articles has in the past three or four years become the most popular weekly in the Soviet Union, and its readership has increased over tenfold. One recent article which aroused a great deal of interest was an interview with your prime minister, Margaret Thatcher, who complained to our correspondent how hard it was to govern a democratic country, and spoke of the discipline which this imposed on citizens and government alike.

We are not yet used to this kind of discipline, but *Ogonyok*'s renewal has been as a result of the new, mutually demanding relationship that now exists between our government and its citizens. Nowadays our government does not always smash the mirrors which present it with a less than flattering image of itself, and the new press law which is soon to be passed will provide us with even greater security in which to work. In any case, we very much value our good name and the good name of our work, and we very much want you to understand us and to rejoice in the new openness and freedom in our home, which is part of the common home of humanity.

Vitaly Korotich

Introduction
Cathy Porter

The weekly illustrated magazine *Ogonyok* ('Flame') has been published in Moscow since 1923. During the Brezhnev era it became a byword for dull journalism. For decades, there were no internal problems or problems of history, no planes crashed, no ships sank. Available at hairdressers, clinics, and airports, *Ogonyok* was popular mainly for its crossword puzzles, representing nobody and offending nobody.

All this changed in 1986, a year after Mikhail Gorbachev was elected General Secretary of the Communist Party and the government embarked on its mighty task of political regeneration. The sudden availability of information opened up vast new areas of investigation and discussion, and *Ogonyok*, under its new editor, Vitaly Korotich, entered the political battle in support of perestroika and the new mood of hope in the country. 'It's time for people calmly to read the papers and accept them as a possible version of the truth,' said Korotich.

Within a year, the magazine's circulation had doubled to a million, and in three years sales had trebled to over three million. Readers' letters increased from twenty to eight hundred a day, and 60 per cent of people in a recent Soviet opinion poll voted *Ogonyok* their favourite publication.

Ogonyok is now a leading commentator on the political, historical, and cultural scene, and represents the very best of glasnost journalism. The writing has gained confidence, going further, exploring more contradictions, and taking more risks, its often slangy idiom well suited to the raw realism of its subject-matter. The artwork too has become increasingly strong, with pictures of Lenin replaced by complex and interesting works of modern Soviet art, photography, and political montage.

Although the army is still a subject that is treated with caution, as are any issues which it is felt might inflame nationalist feelings, the scope of *Ogonyok*'s interests is extremely broad, and includes articles of investigative journalism and historical research, culture, art and photo-journalism, poetry, letters, and excerpts from recent major Soviet and Western fiction. All this is organised fairly haphazardly, but it is this haphazardness which makes *Ogonyok* so exciting, as though pieces were simply pouring in, unable to wait for the 'right' time to be printed.

The magazine is produced in Moscow, takes ten days to print, and may take up to a month to reach the Far Eastern regions of the Soviet Union. Since it is virtually impossible to get topical articles out quickly and to follow them up week by week, news published is no longer 'hard' news, and many articles take the form of extended essays, 4,000 to 5,000 words long, which can still be relevant several months later.

Because I wanted this book to cover as wide a range of subjects as possible, I have edited and cut a number of the articles here, sometimes quite drastically. With some other pieces it has been necessary to amplify and explain for the benefit of readers unfamiliar with the context and background. I have tried to make the selection as representative as possible, however, with articles on Afghanistan, Nagorno-Karabakh, and the Armenian earthquake; national minorities, abandoned babies, and child labour; bribery, stagnation, and the drug trade; prison-camps, sexual delinquency, and the black market; suicide, alcoholism, and mental illness. There are few articles by women on sexuality, the double burden, and discrimination at work, yet there have been interesting articles on the maternity services, and the country's abortion policies come under savage attack by a doctor in 'When There's No Choice'.

Glasnost has exposed the Tsarist and Stalinist legacy of anti-Semitism in Soviet life, but it has also given freedom of speech to anti-Semites. *Ogonyok* has attacked the various quasi-fascistic organisations like Pamyat ('Memory') now appearing on the scene, and articles such as 'A Haunting Spectre' trace the background to the frightening new brand of Great-Russian chauvinism which is attempting to strangle Soviet political life. Pamyat leaders have retaliated by denouncing the magazine as the mouthpiece for an unholy alliance of Freemasons, Zionists, and Satan himself, and meetings addressed by Korotich have been disrupted by bellowing, hair-pulling, and anti-Semitic catcalls. These fierce and often violent confrontations came to a head in 1988, when nationalist groups blocked his candidature to the new Congress of People's Deputies.

Ogonyok has contributed to the process of historical reconstruction now under way in the Soviet Union by publishing major articles on the Stalinist terror, the trauma of collectivisation, and the moral degeneration of the Brezhnev era. It is committed to 'rebuilding the brains of the country', and has republished the writings of Nikolai Bukharin, campaigning for him and other leading persecuted party figures to be rehabilitated. It describes the hardships endured by many outstanding cultural figures, living and dead. In articles like 'The "Lokhankin Phenomenon"' it campaigns to restore the reputation of the intelligentsia. And it testifies to the recent cultural renaissance which has made popular heroes of previously maligned composers and dramatists such as Anatolii Vasilev and Alfred Schnittke.

Yet *Ogonyok* speaks not just for the country's intellectuals, but for anyone who is politically educated and aware. It exposes the close links between organised crime and the corrupt government apparatus ('Under Siege'). It describes the stirrings of change in the factories and mines ('The Square of Suffering'). And it records the nationalist tremors in Siberia, Armenia, the Baltic, and the Far North, which have revealed the bankruptcy of the local government leadership ('Special Region' and 'Arctic Silence?').

Ogonyok speaks too for the millions of ordinary men and women who vanished into Stalin's camps never to be heard of again, and to those who regarded it as their civic duty to inform on their friends. Above all it is looking for documentary evidence of the terror, and as one of the leading sponsors of the Soviet Memorial, set up in 1988 and dedicated to its victims, it aims to collect memoirs, papers, and letters which will enable ordinary people's stories to be inserted into the reconstruction of Soviet history.

Gorbachev's election as Party Secretary in 1985 was by no means unanimous. The first broadside against the new course came in the spring of 1988, when *Soviet Russia*, the journal of the Communist Party, gave prominent space to an open defence of Stalinism from a reader named Nina Andreeva (see 'Interview with an Anti-Hero'). But Andreeva's political manifesto against perestroika produced the opposite of its desired effect, and the press was deluged with articles in defence of perestroika and glasnost.

That summer, a wide range of issues was debated and voted on with unprecedented openness at the Extraordinary 19th Party Conference. The controversial Boris Yeltsin, dismissed Moscow party chief, was given the floor to explain his position. Regional delegates spoke of pollution, the shortages of goods in the shops, and the slowdown in scientific and technological research. The issues of price fixing and food subsidies were debated, and Gorbachev spoke for a thorough-going reform of the legal system. New rights for the mentally ill were proposed, as well as new laws on the freedom to worship and to set up non-party organisations. The conference voted to limit the length of time high office could be held and to alter the role of the party, and a meeting of the Supreme Soviet shortly afterwards supported proposals for free and open elections to a new legislative body.

Because *Ogonyok* is so clearly identified with the present leadership, it takes many of the criticisms intended for it, and there are many who have called for the magazine to be closed down. There have been numerous attempts to isolate it and curb its circulation, and it has come under especially sustained attack from such publications as *Our Contemporary*, *Young Guard*, and *Moscow*. In early 1989, *Pravda* published a demagogic letter signed by ten prominent cultural figures, attacking *Ogonyok* as the 'scum bubbling on the crust of the mighty stream of renewal'. *Ogonyok* responded with a tirade against *Pravda*, signed by a number of writers including Yevtushenko, and it was supported by other progressive publications such as *Novy Mir* ('New World'), *October*, *Banner*, *Youth*, and *Friend of the Nations*. Gorbachev himself then intervened by calling a meeting of journalists and pleading for 'unilateral disarmament'.

After three years *Ogonyok* is still going strong, but it's now that it is starting to get popular that its problems are really starting. This is why all contributors are asked to sign every fact and figure they write, and one mistake will bar them from writing for the magazine again.

The seriousness of the opposition to perestroika is proof of the seriousness of the changes being attempted. *Ogonyok*'s continued survival and popularity are inextricably linked to their success, and reading through these two years' issues is like riding on an accelerating roller-coaster and not knowing whether it's going to be derailed. It is impossible to say how successful the present political apparatus will be in tackling its formidable programme of democratisation, economic reform, and national conciliation, or whether it will founder on economic problems. Shortly before the 1989 demonstrations to mark the anniversary of the October Revolution, Gorbachev took *Ogonyok* and various other radical publications to task for criticising the slow pace of change, and at any time between now and this book's publication there could be major workers' or nationalist disturbances which could provoke a serious political crisis.

As the old certainties collapse, *Ogonyok*'s exposure of evils previously hidden from view is helping to set the preconditions for change. The cumulative effect of so much criticism and self-criticism often makes painful reading. Yet as the Soviet people come to grips with the terror and stagnation of their past, *Ogonyok*'s message of blood, sweat, and tears comes as the galvanising truth needed to make a better future.

November 1989

Look About You!
Ales Adamovich

By the 1960s and 1970s it was becoming possible to explore some of
the not so very distant places of Stalinism (which of course were still
terribly distant). So it was that in 1971 Yanka Bryl and I set off on a
kind of 'journalistic landing-party' for the Siberian towns of
Dudinka and Norilsk, on the vast river Enisei.

Dotted amongst the hills and forests of the landscape lay abandoned settlers' villages, and the earth was scabbed and scarred with
graves and camps.

For Bryl and me, the greatest tragedy of those years was the Nazi
genocide. We had travelled all over Byelorussia listening to people
describe how the fascists slaughtered whole families, burned their
villages, and destroyed vast areas of the countryside. We had heard
them discuss the massacre at the village of Khatyn, and we had just
compiled a book called *From the Village of Fire*. So when a certain
captain invited us into the cabin of his ship to talk to us, we naturally
expected him to go into the sort of terrible details we already had on
our tape-recorders.

'I made dozens of journeys,' he told us. 'On the way out the holds
were full, and on the way back they were empty. I've seen people,
and I've seen what you'd call non-people.'

Sitting with the captain was the director of Dudinka port, who
seemed to understand perfectly what he was talking about. But we
were still puzzled.

'You mean the Germans, or the Vlasovites after the war?' we asked
him.

'No. This was from 1937 until the outbreak of war. After that I
went to the front, and other people took over.'

We know now that the journey into Stalinism doesn't always mean
going somewhere and returning. It also involves us in looking into
ourselves. We have reclaimed a great deal over the past thirty years,

Anti-Stalin demonstration in Kurapaty

yet we still have so much more to squeeze out, drop by bloody drop. For we are all still victims of the phrase 'They wouldn't arrest people for nothing!' and the illusion that those who tortured and slaughtered our people before and after the war did so more 'humanely' and with more justification than did the invaders from the west.

A certain writer I met in Dudinka considered that interests of state justified any crime. 'But they believed in it!' he insisted, referring to the secret police and their boss, whose watchtowers loomed over the heads of his 170 million subjects. But the fascists who committed unspeakable atrocities in occupied Byelorussia, the Ukraine, Russia, and the Baltic also talked about the 'symbols of their belief', and this was exactly how they justified themselves at the Nuremberg trials.

I can remember something of my own enlightenment. It started when I was a partisan during the war, and I saw much that was admitted officially at the 20th Party Congress. Later I read stories and memoirs of the Soviet camps, and I got hold of Solzhenitsyn's *Ivan Denisovich* and Aldan-Semyonov's *Sculpture on the Rock*. I suppose we knew most of it already, yet every page stripped us of yet more of our illusions. I had seen the Germans driving Soviet prisoners into slave labour, but these new discoveries shocked and terrified me. How could our own people kill the weak and shoot people for trying to escape?

We could have asked ourselves what happened to all the millions of prisoners who were driven into exile throughout the thirties. Yet we did everything we possibly could *not* to ask, and we couldn't even admit it when people came back from there and talked about it. I remember talking to an old worker from the glass-factory in my native village of Glusha, where eighty-five prisoners, most of them workers, were sent to the Gulag in 1937. He sobbed as he described how his interrogators had shouted 'Sign that, you bastard!' and squeezed him in 'a man's most painful parts'.

And so we clutched at our illusions, and were unable to admit the truth, either to ourselves or to others. 'I know, I know,' we'd say. 'But they were our people. And Stalin wasn't all bad.'

Those of us who live in or around Minsk have only recently discovered that throughout the thirties people weren't only dying on the Arctic Circle but on our own back doorstep. At first there were the 'social aliens', then the 'kulaks', and then whole professions – engineers, teachers, soldiers, veterans, and party workers – in the general category of 'enemies of the people'. Thousands of people in

Minsk would lie awake listening for the arrival of a car and wondering who would be taken next, and those in the surrounding villages couldn't sleep for the sound of shooting.

After the war my family moved to Minsk, where people remembered absolutely nothing about Kurapaty. The trees had been cut down and had grown again, and the earth had settled over the deep mass graves. These graves were exactly like the ones the Germans left behind when they retreated from places they had occupied. Yet all this had happened *after* the war.

Someone, frightened by the judgement of history, must have remembered what we had so obediently forgotten, for in the seventies these graves were desecrated. Then suddenly the Byelorussian newspaper *Literature and Art* published an article entitled 'Kurapaty – the Road of Death', by Zenon Poznyak, Evgenii Shmygalyov, and Vasilii Bykov, about the excavations being carried out there this May.

From this article we learned that in the pine-forests of Kurapaty, just beneath the grassy dunes where families relax and picnic with their children, lie the bullet-riddled bones and skulls of a monstrous concealed crime. Here lie over 500 mass graves, containing thousands and thousands of bodies. This is why the earth around there is so dented and buckled.

We cracked jokes after the 20th Party Congress (we even managed to joke after Chernobyl!) about the conduct expected of a Soviet citizen crushed to death by the pole of his own banner. Who knows if the mechanism of oblivion will take over here too?

But the time has come to remember. According to Ray Bradbury, the time will come when we remember so much that we shall dig the deepest grave in the world. Those who desecrated the Kurapaty graves in the seventies desecrated our memories, and the memories of generations to come. We must not allow our memory ever to be desecrated again, however much some might want this.

And there are still many who do. They try to soothe our consciences with references to historical precedents (all revolutions devour their own children) and patriotism (we should love everything that is ours), and they even blame the atrocities between 1929 and 1933 on those whom Stalin in his madness finally caught up with in 1937.

Yet we shouldn't be surprised. This was the logic used in 1970 to justify the destruction of 80 per cent of our Byelorussian writers –

like the prudent housewife thinning her carrot bed for a healthier crop.

What a tolerance we had for the intolerable in those days! It should hardly surprise us that perestroika advances in such a zigzag fashion.

The monument in Moscow to the victims of Stalinist repression is a great thing. So what must we do about Kurapaty?

The moment the newspaper published its incontrovertible evidence of the massacres, people started studying the material and archival research work began. There were new appeals for witnesses from the surrounding villages, and a government commission was set up. But people attending a meeting called to discuss this commission expressed their dissatisfaction with its composition and secrecy, and demanded that it include Vasilii Bykov, whose integrity and objectivity they trusted. The desecrated graves yielded a number of things which were carefully scrutinised, and the local prosecutor opened criminal proceedings to identify the remains of the bodies – apparently the first such investigation in our history of a crime committed by the State.

But how many Kurapatys have there been in the other republics? What of the 'capitals' of the Gulag – at Magadan, Vorkuta, Dudinka, and Norilsk? And what of my native town of Glusha, where a third of all the glass-blowers disappeared before the war into the icy clutches of the Gulag?

Where can we take our memories, our flowers, and our pain? Where else but to the place of the crime? To the monument commemorating the 102 Glusha workers who died fighting at the front or with the partisans we must now add these eighty-five names. For these eighty-five are victims of another war – the genocidal war of the dictator.

Grief and pain attend our every step, our every breath and memory. This is the legacy of the Stalin cult. So it will be no surprise for the monster's many still vocal admirers that people all over the country are now building these memorials to their idol, and that in Kurapaty we now have a memorial research centre similar to the one in Moscow.

If we do not understand our own history, we cannot hope to advance towards a new legal, democratic society. The historian and archaeologist Zenon Poznyak, who first drew our attention to Kurapaty and is now leading the investigation, is tenaciously seeking the truth. It's people like him who will make perestroika work.

Excavated remains of Stalin's victims in Kurapaty

Stalin's election propaganda to the huntsmen

Another significant thing is that one single event should have so completely transformed our lives and the pace of perestroika. It's important too that it should all have happened in Minsk, where some of our leading social scientists and ideologists have recently earned the town the reputation of an anti-perestroika Vendée.

The old guard still feel themselves to be in control. Many of those who were rehabilitated after the 20th Party Congress started purging their own ranks after the 27th, and at various round-table meetings after Kurapaty they have been expounding their stale accusations to the leading lights of Byelorussian culture and writing.

But now these people are on the way out.

Thousands of villagers recently walked along the highway to attend a meeting in Kurapaty, with old women carrying candles and young people bearing banners that read 'Stalin – kat [hangman]'. But of course our leaders knew as usual what was best for these people, and they were halted by a row of buses. 'There's a meeting there,' they were told. 'Why don't we take you off to a nice show instead?'

It's a mortal blow for our 'philosophers' that the debate is being taken on to the streets. While ordinary people march under banners saying 'Stalin the hangman', these ideologists read and applaud the report 'Stalin the leader'. Anyone who has ever heard them addressing a meeting these days will know what pathetic figures they are.

The meeting at Kurapaty was organised by young people from various 'informal' political circles, who conducted the proceedings with a tact and sensitivity remarkable for their years. And it was these young people who prevented the old guard from being ignominiously thrown out of the hall.

Kurapaty cannot coexist with this Vendée for much longer. Look about you! The past is waiting for us to discover it. Only when we do so can we fight for the future, and for a just and truly popular socialism. Let us have faith that we can.

Ashes in Polythene:
Some Melancholy Reflections
Vitaly Vitaliev

There are two conditions of human existence which none of us can avoid: birth and death, joy and grief, creation and extinction.

We have learnt to measure a society's economic growth by means of figures, percentages, and statistics. But what about our moral development? The best criterion for this may perhaps be our attitude to the dead.

DUE TO LACK OF CASKETS
ASHES WILL BE DELIVERED IN POLYTHENE BAGS

This announcement is not some sort of sick joke, but appeared not so long ago on the door of a crematorium in the Ukraine.

It was here a few years ago that I said farewell to a dear friend. Through a leaden pall of grief I watched the brisk young crematorium attendant stammering through the official words written out on one piece of paper, while referring back to another piece for this particular client's 'personal details'.

'What is this unpleasant stranger doing here?' I wondered. 'And why is he saying these things?'

On his right arm the brisk young man wore a red and black band depicting a flame, and on his chest he wore a metal badge with another flame on it. And for some reason we dignify this appalling vulgarity as a 'ritual' . . .

When we returned to the crematorium a few days later for the ashes, we had to hand over all our money before they would give us the casket. (There were evidently enough of them to go round then.)

I then had to go to the cemetery office to get permission to bury it. Behind the door of the room marked Director sat a woman with dyed blonde hair and fat fingers loaded with rings. A red triangular pennant above her bore the words: FIRST PRIZE FOR SOCIALIST

COMPETITION. A more glaring example of the bureaucratisation of the soul would be hard to imagine.

Another good man, a labour veteran and war invalid, died recently in another southern town. He died during a public holiday – death being no respecter of such occasions – and what made it so terrible was not merely that his family was plunged into grief at a time of general merrymaking, but that because of the celebrations it was impossible for his sons to find a coffin, and they had to travel around the whole of the Donetsk region in search of one. Even when they eventually found one, however, their ordeal wasn't over. The funeral procession arrived at the cemetery to be told that a huge boulder had suddenly appeared in the grave, and that the grave-diggers would need a hundred roubles to remove it. Since it seemed hardly proper to haggle at a cemetery, they agreed, and the boulder presumably moved on to another grave.

I remember arriving with a friend one blazing July day at the Pathological Anatomy Department (i.e. the mortuary) of Moscow's First City Hospital, to collect the body of his father, a well-known film actor. In the hall of this dismal place was a sign executed in gilded letters:

CORPSES ARE AVAILABLE ONLY ON RECEIPT OF
DEATH CERTIFICATE AND PASSPORT
BEARING RESIDENCE PERMIT

For some reason this put me in mind of the sign I once saw outside the building of the Moscow Olympics organising committee:

FANTA IS AVAILABLE ONLY BETWEEN THE HOURS OF
14.00 AND 16.00

What is going on? What kind of spiritual corpse can have written this sign? Has no one noticed its barbarous insensitivity? Have they forgotten that there are *living* people in this mortuary?

From the mortuary we were driven in one of Moscow's yellow hearses, with its strict No Smoking signs, to the Nicholas Archangel cemetery near the little town of Reutov.

A long queue of yellow hearses was waiting outside the crematorium, and dominating everything else was a tall chimney, belching out clouds of thick black smoke. At the sight of this smoke several women in the queue collapsed in a faint.

When our turn finally came we were led into a hall by a woman in a mouse-grey dress. 'Exactly ten minutes for the final farewells,' she snapped.

A lot of people – students, colleagues, and admirers – were waiting to speak at the dead man's coffin . . . Suddenly an organ pealed out from under the roof of the hall, and gazing up into the gallery I could see a gloomy man pedalling away oblivious to everyone below.

By the time he had finished we had lost exactly half of our allotted time. And exactly five minutes later, the woman in the mouse-grey dress popped up again beside the coffin and declared the final farewells to be over. Her professional mask of grief was now replaced by an expression of open hatred, as though saying 'Shut up and get on with it!'

We made our way out of the crematorium, stopping first to make way for another funeral procession, and there under the blazing July sun we saw thousands of grieving, living people queuing up for their turn. There was nowhere to shelter from the sun or sit down, and the only thing to drink was a trickle of warm, rusty water from a hosepipe on the ground. Plainly no one had considered the basic comforts of the living mourners. Yet hanging on the fence above this concentration of human grief was a poster advertising the 'comfort' of burying the casket in a 'closed columbarium'.

The Funeral March rang out. Hearses kept arriving at the gates. Then all of a sudden the sticky air exploded with gunshots. In one of the crematorium halls some military top brass was taking his leave of this life, and the guard of honour was letting off a salvo in his honour. Dazed by the heat, the crowds shuddered convulsively at the sound of the shots, and the black smoke belched forth into the sky . . .

I don't want to demand punishment for slapdash cemetery attendants, or to make suggestions as to the reorganisation of the 'ritual service', or even to name the crooks who profit from human grief (for those who speculate in death are beyond reach).

I simply want to say:

Indifference to the dead is a terrible disease. Unless we root it out we shall never build a genuinely democratic society. For democracy means compassion, and compassion means respect for the dead.

Down with the insult of polythene for ashes! Away with idiotic signs! Remove boulders from graves! Conceal crematorium chimneys from sight! Let us behave like human beings! Are we alive, or are we all dead?

P.S. After this article had gone to press, the editors received the price-list displayed at one Moscow crematorium: '. . . Cremation of children: one body – 0.67 kopecks . . .'

The spiritual blasphemy continues . . .

About Sausage
Pyotr Aleshkovsky

Long suburban trains roll every day into Moscow from Kaluga, Ryazan, Dmitrov, Serpukhov, and Zvenigorod, and hordes of people alight driven by the single-minded desire to buy sausage.

These 'sausage trains' have become a central part of our lives. People keep on coming, cheerfully using up their holidays or taking days off work. 'It's not so bad, we're used to it!' they say. 'What's a day wasted when you're stocked up with sausage for the next fortnight!'

Yet they don't look happy. They look tense and tired as they anticipate the queues and the angry shouts of 'Here come the country bumpkins, cleaning out the shops!' They can think of nothing to say in their own defence as they stuff the sausage into their hold-alls like thieves, praying that the saleswoman won't notice them as they anxiously creep off to the next queue.

We Muscovites also queue up meekly, buy what we need, and scuttle off home. We have grown so used to it that we rarely stop to question why it should be so, and I wouldn't have given it a second thought either, had I not become involved in a story which involves not merely the 'sausage trains' or the shortages, but the far larger issue of our servility, our willingness to tolerate the intolerable, our lack of confidence, and the terrible exhaustion this engenders.

On the afternoon of 19 February, we had a call at the *Ogonyok* office from a man named Vladimir Shakhgeldyants, from the Uryupin meat-processing plant. 'Come over here and look at my sausage,' he said. 'I swear there's nothing wrong with it, but they've deliberately destroyed it because Moscow doesn't want it!'

Intrigued by the idea of an unwanted sausage in Moscow, I arranged to meet him, then hurried off to my local shop.

'There's no point getting involved in all this, you'll never get to the bottom of it,' the manager advised me, but he attempted nonetheless to explain. 'It's almost impossible to sell boiled smoked sausage at 9 roubles 50 kopecks a kilogram, and it's only bought by people from out of town, who need to store meat for a long time. People in the capital won't touch it. They'll grab the uncooked stuff without even looking at the price. But the 9.50 sausage is poor quality and much too expensive. It's got to the point now where I'm being forced to buy it. If I agree to take say a ton, they'll make up my stocks with something else, which is in short supply. We can always offload it on to the factories or people's voucher packets – veterans, teachers, and so on. They moan, but they take it . . .'

The manager suddenly broke off, remembering that he was talking to someone from the press, then he shrugged and went on.

'But the main problem, as I see it, is that we've lost the art of trading. People would gladly buy the boiled sausage if the authorities decided to lower the price. They certainly bought it when it cost four roubles.'

I sympathised with the manager's pessimism. Whom can these kinds of commercial practices possibly benefit? And why on earth did the price suddenly shoot up? I still didn't know the answers to these questions. But the story of what I had assumed to be a straightforward commercial conflict of interests soon acquired a quite different character.

Shortly before Shakhgeldyants's telephone call, a lorry from the Uryupin meat-processing plant had unloaded 6.9 tons of boiled-smoked sausage at Moscow's 14th Cold Store. Later, when I went down to the cold store to watch the vans unload, I saw there a number of illustrated posters, including one of Leopold the ginger cat, issuing his familiar cry: 'Why can't we all be friends!' Whom this cartoon character was meant to be addressing was not clear, but I appreciated the drivers' sense of humour. At the time, however, the dashing young man in the driver's seat of the Uryupin meat lorry merely sat preening himself as if to say: 'Just you wait!'

It seemed now that all the cold store had to do was to deliver the sausage to the shops. But this was not to be. Checks carried out in its labs revealed that the sausage contained 39.4 per cent moisture, 1.4 per cent higher than allowed by the State Meat Board. The cold store, which stood to lose almost 1,000 roubles if it tried to dry the sausage out, immediately fired off a threatening telegram to the Uryupin plant, announcing: 'The sausage is substandard.'

'We can't go on like this,' said Vladimir Shakhgeldyants. 'We've sunk to the level of the proletariat who have nothing to lose but our chains, only these chains are unbreakable. The State Meat Board is the only wholesale meat consumer in the country. They have the sole right to buy and distribute meat, and they order us to produce expensive sausage for Moscow. We carry out their orders, but those under them, such as the cold store, just write off every load we send them. It's much easier for them to write off the sausage than to rethink things. Personally I'd be happy to sell that sausage in Uryupin. It's not often we get any sausage at all in the shops there these days.'

I soon knew all the details of the Uryupin story. I learned about the chemist and the doctor summoned by telegram to the cold store, and about how their request to take part in a second analysis of the sausage's moisture content was turned down. I learned about the arbitrary moisture analysis performed by the Trading Commission in the laboratory of the State Meat Board. And I saw for myself the laughably named 'Moscow' sausage, which comes from all over the country to the wholesalers in the capital, who are apparently the only people who want it.

What is so extraordinary is that if the cold store is deliberately spoiling perfectly edible sausage, as Vladimir Shakhgeldyants assures me it is, it is sabotaging the very system it has itself created. Sabotaging it passively, of course, with methods left over from the old system, but sabotaging it nonetheless, like the monster devouring its own tail.

'It's a dirty business,' Shakhgeldyants declared at our first meeting. 'I don't know who benefits from "spoiling" a perfectly good product.' Shakhgeldyants thought it must be the work of a commercial mafia organisation, whereas I tended to see it as a typical case of economic bungling. But we were both determined to act.

We went first to the Moscow People's Inspectorate, where we were immediately admitted to see Galina Vodovozova, director of the food and light industry department. I posed as a worker at the Uryupin plant, since I wanted an insider's view of the case. But Galina Vodovozova didn't merely listen to us, she was even human.

'If this is true, there'll be criminal charges to answer,' she said, and promised to set up an impartial investigation.

Fortified by her support, we set off to the State Meat Board, the

Government Office of Trading Standards, the Trade Commission, the 14th Cold Store, and the Department of Trade and Agriculture. To our amazement, they all agreed to see us. They all spoke sympathetically of Moscow's sausage 'glut', and all of them, apart from the Meat Board, were prepared to take our word for it that the sausage was well up to the standards required. I was beginning to get the impression that none of it was new to any of them . . .

During a highly confidential conversation at the Department of Trade and Agriculture (where my assumed identity came into its own), one exceptionally frank official confessed: 'We've had problems with this sausage ever since the price went up.'

'So who ordered the price rise?' I asked.

The official put on a solemn face, and jabbed his finger at the ceiling. 'The price has remained the same for the Uryupin plant and the cold store, and the difference is channelled straight into our budget, to cover our losses on vodka sales. What can we do?' He winked at me. 'You'd think there'd be nothing simpler than bringing the price down to seven roubles, and adding the two left over to the price of the uncooked sausage. But oh no, *they* wouldn't dream of changing their minds – which of course leaves *you* up the creek.'

He winked at me again, more sympathetically this time.

What these 'secret instructions' were I never discovered. Other people we met were less talkative, and simply passed us on with an apologetic smile to someone else, so that were it not for Shakhgeldyants's iron determination and the support of the Moscow Inspectorate, we would have got nowhere.

'That sausage is substandard. Take it back at once before it's ruined,' we were told by the cold store's manager, V. P. Yegorov. Yegorov proved most reluctant to get involved, since he was simply biding his time before moving upwards as vice-director of the Moscow regional department of the Meat Board. He is there now, and has done his utmost to obstruct our investigation. Once he even urged us in friendly tones to sell the sausage at Uryupin. 'They'll snap it up,' he assured us, thus unwittingly confirming that the sausage was quite edible, and could be sold.

One can feel some sympathy for the man, for to this day he hasn't been authorised to regrade the sausage. It might establish a precedent, after all, as happened with fish, whose price is now allowed to drop 30 per cent if it's perfectly edible but not of the very highest quality.

Yegorov knew quite well that it would be a criminal offence to sell the sausage without special authorisation from the Meat Board. He knew that this sausage won't be found in the shops or stalls of the town in which it's produced. And he knew that the Meat Board would never consent to 'substandard' sausage being sold. Yet he was obviously mortified by the whole business and desperate to wash his hands of it. Whoever would have thought that the demoralised Uryupin plant would decide to fight back?

'Why are you putting my back to the wall?' Shakhgeldyants shouted, after Yegorov had urged us to 'leave in peace'.

'Are you speaking to me?' the manager said, answering his question with another. He had just been summoned to the phone from the People's Inspectorate, and was now making a last-ditch attempt to save the honour of his firm . . .

Time passed, and around the middle of March a nice girl named Valya arrived to decorate my flat. Valya came from a village near Pereslavl. When I told her about my sausage saga, she said: 'I never buy sausage in Moscow now, it's far too dear. I used to buy it, though, when it was four roubles a kilo.'

'But would they buy it at nine roubles in the country?' I asked.

'They'll buy any old rubbish in the country – we hardly ever *get* any sausage. Cutlets which cost twelve kopecks here cost us twenty-four. Dumplings are twice the price too, and they're all frozen together . . .'

I felt so ashamed that on 23 March I decided to attend the last session of the Moscow People's Inspectorate, and to share some of this 'popular wisdom' with Pavel Anatolevich Kuznetsov, the State Meat Board's director.

'What's Pereslavl got to do with it?' said Comrade Kuznetsov in bewilderment. 'How did it all start? You should have come to me in the first place. I would have immediately sold off this sausage in the Moscow provinces, and used up all the stocks . . .'

I am sure this affair has nothing to do with some commercial mafia, and everything to do with our bureaucratic system, unwieldy, uncommercial, and able only to carry out someone else's uncoordinated, undemocratic decisions. This system is a disastrous anachronism in the current era of perestroika, but is fiercely attached to the past and determined to give up none of its hard-won gains.

On One Side, and On the Other . . .
Yury Tyurin

I have before me a tear-off calendar for the year 1989, 300 million copies of which are issued by the Political Publishing House. The page for December shows a portrait of Stalin, with the inscription: 'Communist Party activist'. The other side of the page continues: '. . . Prominent member of the Communist Party, the Soviet government, and the international Communist and workers' movement . . .' Further on we read: 'The novelty and complexity of the problems in these years revealed the extreme contradictions of this political figure . . .'

So *that* explains the 'contradictions' of the bloody dictator who murdered and mutilated millions of his people! All this, explain the editors, was a 'departure from the Leninist principles of party and government life'. What they don't explain, however, is that the Stalin cult is something totally alien to socialism, and has had a catastrophic effect on our country's socialist development and creative potential.

Are the editors not disturbed by the 'theoretical basis' for Stalin's politics of mass repression? His concept of sharpening the class struggle as the means to make society advance along the socialist path?

The editors must have read his speech at the February 1937 party plenum 'On the inadequacies of party work and the measures needed to liquidate the Trotskyists and other double-dealers'. 'The more we advance and the more successful we are,' he stated, 'the more will the embittered remnants of the smashed exploiting classes slander the Soviet government, and the more violent will their struggle become . . .' And further on: '. . . The enemies of the people will double-cross us, disguising themselves as Bolsheviks and party members in order to worm their way into our organisations and gain our trust . . .'

In a section of his speech entitled 'Our Task', Stalin gave direct orders to carry out mass repressions. 'The wrecker must enjoy occasional successes in his job, for that is the only way he can keep our trust and carry on with his wrecking work . . . I think this question is clear and needs no further explanation.' And 1937 had only just started . . .

Some of those at the plenum, such as Nikolai Bukharin, didn't return, and before long the Stalin–Yezhov machine had swung into action and the conveyor belt of death was in full swing.

As a 'prominent member of the international Communist and workers' movement' (see above), Stalin also did enormous damage to the Communist parties of the Communist International by unceremoniously meddling in their internal affairs. The Political Publishing House could not fail to know about the leaders of the Austrian, Hungarian, German, Polish, Romanian, Finnish, Latvian, Lithuanian, and Estonian Communist parties who disappeared into the maw of the terror machine, and the prominent members of the international Communist and workers' movement who were murdered by the Stalin–Yezhov guillotine.

But the idea I find hardest to accept is that it was the 'novelty and complexity of the problems' which accounted for the insane crimes committed by Stalin and his associates. No, he achieved what he did by abandoning the principles of collective leadership and democracy in the party, destroying the spirit of party comradeship, and perverting its conferences and congresses – and by his own inflated self-esteem and his contempt for other people's opinions.

As we resurrect truth and democracy and create a system which will ensure that these mistakes are not repeated, we must examine the past, and check everything we do against Engels's warning to stop treating party officials with such excessive reverence, humbly begging their forgiveness as blameless bureaucrats. They are not. They are merely our servants.

Timberworks
Vitaly Eryomin

> . . . And begged mercy for the fallen.
>
> A. S. Pushkin

I

The remote northern regions of Komi, in the Adjar Autonomous Republic, with its dense forests, impenetrable swamps and non-existent roads, provide the perfect natural conditions for the isolation of dangerous criminals in strict-regime camps. In some places the camps have no fences or barbed wire, for even if you did try to make a run for it you wouldn't get far.

The prisoners work mainly in the open, hewing and gathering timber. Life is hard. The winters are freezing cold and the summers bring clouds of mosquitoes. But the most oppressive thing about the place is its remoteness, buried in the depths of the taiga across thirty-eight vast regions of the country. Not every prisoner's life companion will make the two or three annual visits allowed her by law, for the expense is great and the journey long.

One former camp inmate wrote a letter promising to abandon his thieving ways if only they sent him somewhere not so far north. Yet many prisoners serve their term here only to commit another crime, generally more serious than the last, knowing full well that they'll be sent straight back to Komi.

'OK,' I said to one veteran prisoner. 'Forget the people you've robbed, aren't you at least sorry for yourself?'

'Yes, I am,' he admitted, to my surprise. 'This place turns us into animals.'

The morning we arrived at the Komi camp, a prisoner had got into the Restricted Zone, gone up to within twenty yards of the watchtower, thrown his shackles at the guard, and showered him

with curses. It hadn't taken long for the nineteen-year-old soldier to lose his patience . . .

The military prosecutor ordered the trial to start at once. Yet he was unable to explain, even had he wanted to, what had impelled a twenty-seven-year-old prisoner with a six-year sentence to this fatal step.

Komi's forest camps are not merely a vast criminal isolator, but also a vast accumulator of insults and hatred. The harder a prisoner's conditions and the longer his sentence, the more his behaviour is determined by the elemental instinct of self-preservation. Some exaggerate minor ailments, some openly malinger, some refuse to work giving no reason at all.

Some work for the bosses. Others get out of general chores by elbowing their way into administrative jobs. Another group pass themselves off as important figures in the criminal underworld. But all, according to their strength, intelligence, and villainy, seek ways to ease their situation.

Each camp has its elite and its proletariat – the 'sloggers'. The prisoners' official power is their soviet; their unofficial power is that of the 'wreckers'. The 'wreckers', and the 'sloggers' who support them, refuse to collaborate in any way with the authorities, and are on bad terms with those who do.

Camp society has its own concepts of what a prisoner can and cannot do. He'd be asking for it if he worked in the Restricted Zone, wrote a complaint, or was a witness in any judicial or administrative investigation. But the greatest crime of all is any sort of secret denunciation or open appeal to the staff.

Within camp society the demands of each individual prisoner are generally in conflict with those of the administration, and each day is filled with the contradictions between these two powers and two codes of behaviour. The staff have a vast arsenal of punishments at their command, which make the existence of the mutinous 'wrecker' even harder. This then enables the 'wrecker' to appear a victim of arbitrary authority, allowing him to acquire his own negative authority over the other prisoners.

'We only bother with the "wreckers" and the co-operative ones. We haven't time for the ones in the middle,' says Colonel Pryakhin, governor at Komi, thus unintentionally defining the aims of all the authorities' practical rehabilitation work amongst the prisoners.

2

It is a rainy summer at Komi, and after each downpour the staff has orders to dig up twenty centimetres of earth around the entire fence of the Restricted Zone. Convicts are officially spared this heavy labour, and it remains the responsibility of the authorities. But they hate messing around in the Zone, and try to persuade the prisoners to do it for them.

'Digging up the Zone is a real torture for us, and the Corrective Labour Code says we can only use prisoners' unpaid labour to build public amenities in their place of confinement,' said Pryakhin. 'A lot of prisoners are at loggerheads with the soldiers anyway, remember. The "wreckers" are terrified to go into the Restricted Zone and they all despise this work.'

'I'd rather die than go into the Zone' are words the administration hears almost every day. They react to them according to the terms of the Corrective Labour Code, which states that one of the main methods of punishing prisoners is the 'special regime'. The main requirement of the 'special regime' is unquestioning obedience. This means that it is for the administrators to decide amongst themselves whether an order is legal or not. Unpaid work is illegal, of course, but if the authorities are not obeyed further punishments will follow.

Fortunately the camp also includes officers of the Crime Prevention Squad, who always help out with the digging. It's not nearly as bad as hauling wood, after all. But how many active squad officers are there? we ask. 'Just fifteen,' replies Pryakhin.

The administration sends Crime Prevention Squad officers to the Restricted Zone only when all else fails and everyone else refuses to go. But there are at least a thousand of these others, who stick to the unwritten rules of the Zone. A convict may fulfil his work quotas and go along with the regime, but if he refuses to work in the Zone they'll automatically put him down as a 'wrecker' and pack him off to the 'isolator'.

It is as though the isolator is deliberately intended to force new arrivals into the arms of the 'wreckers' already in there. 'Schizo' is their name for this cold, damp cell, with its concrete walls, its complete lack of bedding ('just your mug under your head and your shoes under your back', some inmates told me), and its reduced food rations (this has been recently amended).

'They lock us up in here like animals,' they told me. And yet the air wouldn't be so foul in a cowshed, a pigsty, or a kennel, for there at least they wouldn't batten down the windows so tightly. 'You should smoke less!' one of their epauletted masters advises them cheerfully. One of the convicts goes to the lavatory, opens it up, and calmly demonstrates what he thinks of the smiling commander in the doorway.

Those in 'Schizo' are generally there for insulting the staff. For this you'll get your name taken. And once that happens you can get fifteen days inside for not buttoning up your shirt collar or tidying your locker, or for smoking in the wrong place or talking to your mate in the next hut. A former miner from Vorkuta named Pyotr Koptilkin had just served his twenty-six-year sentence when he lashed out at a guard. He has now spent eighteen months of his second sentence in the Closed Cell, which is even worse than 'Schizo'. And all for 'not letting some bastard parasite call me scum', says Koptilkin.

It's one thing to be sent to 'Schizo' for playing cards, and for this even those most hostile to the authorities will bear no special grudge. But it's quite another to be pulled in for 'setting fire to a snowdrift'. The guards who battle with the 'wreckers' will say they're beating the villainy out of them, not noticing as they puff and pant how ordinary human dignity is getting crushed in the process. One habitué of 'Schizo' managed by some miracle to see his wife as a special concession. 'So you've found yourself a husband, eh!' leered the guard. The woman answered back, her husband chipped in, and instead of a nice meeting-room they both got 'Schizo'. 'Schizo' not only destroys people's health and throws normal 'sloggers' on the mercy of the 'wreckers'. It breeds a terrible hatred for officers of the Crime Prevention Squad.

People are rarely caught with drugs here, as they are in other camps throughout the country, and the 'residents', i.e. the suppliers of alcohol, haven't yet cornered the market in these timber colonies. But God help someone who gets hold of a few potatoes from the outside and bakes them. 'I must bring to your attention', reads a duty officer's memorandum, 'that a certain convict systematically refuses breakfast, and encourages others to follow suit by eating with another convict in the sleeping quarters, thus infringing the hygiene regulations.'

There's no check on these Crime Prevention officers. Many of them are quite brazenly out for their own interests, and only fifteen active Squad officers in this camp do their allotted forestry work. One of them, a man named Shevtsov, raped an under-age girl a few years ago. And is Shevtsov now savouring the bitter taste of captivity? He is not. He is still working in the Squad as a bath attendant. Another man, one Reshetilo, gained the authorities' confidence, was allowed out, and promptly disappeared. None of this would have mattered had Reshetilo been an ordinary member of the Squad, rather than its superintendent.

Most camps we have visited now have new, more liberal directors. But there are still those who spit at the prisoners: 'This won't last long, you'll see! We'll soon get people in to bludgeon you into the ground!'

3

While leafing through the Criminal Code, I found at least two articles of relevance to the 'bludgeoners'. Article 131 states that any deliberate slight to a person's honour and dignity, insultingly expressed, is a criminal offence. Yet according to Article 113, it is not only an offence to beat a prisoner, but to harass them in any way. The idea that Article 113 might stand in the way of the bludgeoners would merely irritate the guards, and produce Homeric laughter from the convicts. Both will say: 'Who are the guards supposed to be responsible for? The prisoners?'

'Mr Governor, sir, prisoner so-and-so reporting his arrival.' These words are heard hundreds of times every day in any colony, and no one finds anything strange in them. The law-breaker is a citizen for the last time in court. After that he becomes a prisoner and is no longer regarded as a human being.

It's because we no longer see the criminal as a citizen that we don't mind his sentence depriving him of his freedom, the chance to see his family, to lead a physically normal life, and to work at the job for which he was trained. Yet because one punishment alone is thought inadequate to force a criminal to repent and reform, additional punishments are added on, which the bludgeoners can turn into instruments of moral and physical torture.

The greater someone's crime, the more society should concern itself with rehabilitating him back to normal life. But in fact the stricter the regime a prisoner is on, the fewer letters he can write to his family, and the fewer visits he receives from his wife and children.

One criminal may need several months to turn a new leaf, another may need years. But none can receive presents and messages before serving half of his sentence. Every criminal routinely has his head shaved, forgoing his normal human appearance for years on end so as to make him easier to catch if he escapes. Those with only a few months of their sentence left to serve are usually allowed to grow their hair, but the minute they commit some minor offence and land up in 'Schizo', the barber is again called in.

Even in the Gulag era, prisoners were allowed to move freely about the camp sector. But during the Brezhnev years, some bright spark had the idea of surrounding every barracks with barbed wire. So-called 'lock-ups' were created, like prisons within a prison, and now you can end up in 'Schizo' just for exchanging a few words with your mate in another barracks. The staff themselves recognise that the lock-ups are unnecessary and merely infuriate the prisoners, but it doesn't change anything.

In the Gulag era, prisoners were stamped with numbers. After all these years, a new method of identification has now been dreamt up whereby each wears a stripe with his name on it. For whose benefit is this? The governor's, maybe? But they know everyone anyway. The guards'? But they too have professional memories. The fact is that no one needs it. It was decided in some important office that these stripes would help to maintain discipline, and that was that.

For many years prisoners were forbidden to consume the strong, tea-like brew known as 'chifir', which was thought to make them aggressive and uncontrollable. The Crime Prevention Squad launched an official round-up of all the chifir-makers, countless prisoners caught with their chifir passed through the 'Schizo' school of criminal conduct, and countless of them received new sentences for non-co-operation. The round-up continued for decades, and was finally called off in 1972. This wasn't marked by any increased criminality, and the tea can now be bought at all the shops in the camps (although no more than a packet a month: even here the bludgeoners have been busy). But how many lives were broken in the process?

'Prisoners receive adequate nourishment to ensure the normal vital functions of the organism,' states the Corrective Labour Code. What is the cost of 'normal nourishment' for those on strict regime? we asked. Twenty roubles a month, we were told. Whilst those in 'Schizo' are allocated 'decreased nutritional norms', amounting to ten roubles a month. When convict Pyotr Koptilkin was carried out of 'Schizo' he weighed just ninety pounds. Even if Koptilkin did break the rules, is this any way to treat a working person? Is it right that he should have to work in the freezing cold consumed by hunger?

Last year this camp made a clear profit of 28 million roubles. Mention this to the prisoners and they won't mince their words about their governor.

'We earn him millions of roubles, and he feeds us on sixty-six kopecks a day. We're supposed to get sixty-five grams of meat, but where is it? The cook was sacked for stealing it, but now he's back. We know food rations are controlled from above, but do they think we'll work our guts out for them, and they can send in others to replace us when we die?'

The prisoners' complete lack of rights is eloquently expressed in the way they refer to the governor as 'boss'. The boss has virtually unlimited power over them. Even if someone writes a complaint, the complaint hits the mark, and the prosecutor makes an inspection, nothing changes. 'I'm not going to feed you. The minister will back me up,' the former vice-governor of one of the colonies told some prisoners in 'Schizo'. And he was quite right. The overriding official concern is that all 'wreckers' should be mercilessly crushed, a struggle which shields all abuses from the authorities. It's not surprising that the prisoners hate the prosecutors as much as they do the most zealous 'bludgeoners'.

'They keep stealing from me!' a convict named Kostryukhov was yelling in Pryakhin's office. 'They owe me 187 roubles, and I can't get my hands on a kopeck of it. I can't even buy a packet of tobacco at the shop. If I didn't work I'd be in "Schizo". But I do work. How do I get paid? It should be at least a rouble a day!'

Pryakhin called in the rate-setter, and they went through Kostryukhov's notes. 'That's not my signature!' he shouted, and backed this up by signing his name next to the forged one. Pryakhin and the rate-setter were at a loss for words . . .

'There's a whole queue of us to see you!' people were shouting to me at the door. 'Why don't you hold an open meeting?'

I'm sure Pryakhin wouldn't have refused me one if I'd asked for it, but the idea terrified me. Who knows how it might have ended?

'Punish him,' Pryakhin was urged by his senior warder after Kostryukhov finally left his office, crimson with rage. A meeting would have ended with many more besides Kostryukhov in 'Schizo' . . .

The dehumanisation of prisoners is particularly marked amongst the soldiers who escort them from place to place. 'We are unarmed,' Pryakhin told me, 'whereas the soldiers are armed, and this turns even the officers' heads.'

'The soldiers are told that a prisoner high on chifir can jump seven yards and breathe fire, and they don't see us as people,' one of the 'sloggers' told me. 'It's about fifteen minutes' walk to the work area, but it often takes us an hour, especially if it's snowing or pouring with rain. The column tries to speed up, the escorting officer gives orders to slow down, those at the front still drag their feet, and the ones at the back pile on top of them. Then the soldiers let the dogs loose on us, fire shots over our heads, and give the order "Sit!" We sit down in the snow or mud and curse at the soldiers, and they curse at us. And all this can happen twice a day.'

When human dignity is so degraded, it's not surprising that life itself is degraded. Every soldier knows you can get ten days' leave for catching someone trying to escape. He also knows that the use of weapons is allowed only in exceptional cases. But why should he bother with any other method if the prisoners aren't even human . . . ?

4

Re-educating, re-forming the personality. Some of us might have been deceived by these words when we read about the convict labourers who constructed the Belomor Canal, but I am sure that no one imprisoned in a labour camp nowadays would talk in such terms. Any such venture here is doomed by both authorities and prisoners alike. A convict occasionally manages to retain something of his humanity by living another life of his own, private and invisible to the 'bludgeoners' and outsiders. But this is a very rare personal achievement, the exception which proves the rule.

But there are no neutral processes here. If the old stereotypes of work with convicts don't yield positive results, what results do they yield?

In Moscow's prisons you have to wait six months to see a dentist. Virtually everyone who spends five or six years stuck out in the depths of Komi will lose half their teeth. By the age of forty, and

often considerably earlier, almost everyone there will have developed a variety of chronic ailments. All timber colonies have separate sleeping barracks for those suffering from tuberculosis, yet they have no separate canteen, and have to eat and work alongside those who are fit.

Those with rampant TB are confined to a special colony, but since doctors tend to regard everyone coming to them as malingerers, the early stages of the disease are often not detected, allowing other prisoners' weakened organisms to be attacked by the bacillus. According to official information, the number of those in labour camps suffering from rampant TB has more than doubled since 1981.

Other, more serious consequences are merely being deferred. Sooner or later the patient will be freed, and he need only travel a few stops in a crowded bus or hang around in a bar to pass on the disease to dozens more unsuspecting people.

This is the price of 'scientifically calculated' food rations in general, and 'reduced rations' in particular. It is the camp doctors' sacred duty to check up on the supplies and quality of the food, and to speak out against the practice of punishing prisoners through their stomachs.

'We have 1,000 cattle, 1,200 pigs and about 10,000 hens,' I was told at the Mikunsk timber manager's office. Yet when we went to the colony, they took us anywhere we wanted but the canteens . . .

Portrait of a
Man of Self-Will
Alla Gerber

At these times when everyone is tapping out ideas at the speed of light for fear they won't have time to say everything they want to, I have remained obstinately silent.

'Have you nothing to say?' my colleagues would ask. But I needed to be silent for a while, to find my own voice. I was like someone robbed of the power of speech by some powerful shock, who needed another to find it again. Perhaps my assignment to interview the theatre director Anatoly Vasilev would serve this purpose: if I couldn't write about him, what could I write about! Not because he's a genius – time alone will tell – but because he is timeless.

'Perestroika is nothing new for me,' Vasilev says. 'Theatre is always an experiment. But theatre also means remaining true to others, despite all obstacles . . .'

Anatoly Alexandrovich Vasilev. Date of birth – about 1942. Parents and nationality – not known. Graduate in organic chemistry from Rostov University. Later joined the navy (or was he conscripted?).

'Vasilev belongs to the sixties generation . . .' I read somewhere. Now I know that's wrong. He belongs to the seventies, and he is that passive, demoralised generation's most fierce and articulate voice. Instead of merely sitting out the wasted years waiting for things to change, he worked (though they tried to stop him), stubbornly maintaining his independence from progressives and conservatives alike.

Vasilev is permanently at war with everything permanent. 'I've always tried as far as possible to destroy, forget, and confuse. Art begins at the point where we leave normality behind.'

It's from this desperate war against time that Vasilev derives his strength. He destroys in the name of creation. His life is unencumbered. 'We're given so little,' he says. 'It's a sin to squander it.'

Vasiliev

His theoretical teachers were Stanislavsky and Meyerhold. As a student at the State Theatre Institute, he had two remarkable teachers in Maria Knebel and Andrei Popov. 'Popov seethed with fertile, life-affirming ideas,' he says. 'And this meant an enormous amount in those years, when life was so degraded by stress.' About Maria Knebel he says: 'She educated not just the director but the whole person, specifically one's relationship with the theatre. More specifically still, one's relationship with art.'

Vasilev had already been involved with the theatre, however, when he ran a student drama group at Rostov University. It was there that he met Victor Slavkin, a member of Mark Rozovsky's Moscow theatre studio Our House.

The history of Our House is closely tied to that of the sixties. It was a community of friends searching, with frequently brilliant results, for a shared life in the theatre. It seemed set to last for ever. Then it all came to an end. But for a long time they believed that they could simply start afresh with new people. These ageing children of the sixties used to meet once a year on their birthday to put on scenes from their old plays, and in these happy moments they imagined that nothing had changed and everything would go on as before.

'Slavkin arrived at our theatre in Rostov from Moscow, and he at once became one of us,' says Vasilev. 'His play *The Elder Daughter of a Young Man* impressed me immediately. I had to put it on before saying goodbye to my youth, as some sort of tribute to it . . .'

Before *The Elder Daughter* Vasilev had staged *Solo for Striking Clock* for the Moscow Art Theatre. Then came the original version of Gorky's play *Vassa Zheleznova*. It was *Vassa* which most clearly demonstrated the basic principles of his methods. The truth for him lies in the silences, the spaces between the words. So that the emotions, the gestures, the air the characters breathe, take possession of an audience, reaching not just their eyes and ears but their very soul.

At rehearsals Vasilev always says: 'Pure ideology and politics don't interest me. You have to learn to act out your surroundings. Atmosphere itself is ideology . . .'

The Elder Daughter is about the sixties, and about people who can't stop time around them, so have stopped it inside their own heads instead. It is the sad tale of old people who are young, and young people who are old; about the first, slightly sentimental conflict between the generations, when young people were no longer in sympathy with their elders, but hadn't yet learnt to hate them. For the older generation then were still pure and honest; pathetic and ridiculous, but proud and free.

For four years *The Elder Daughter* was the most popular play in Moscow. 'I was trapped,' says Vasilev. 'This is what success means. Being unable to break away from the things you need to put behind you. Then Victor Slavkin told me his ideas for a new play called *I'm Forty, But I Look Young*. At the time I thought it was a typical scenario of arrival, infatuation, and disappointment. But then the play appeared as *Serso*, and two years later I returned to it. I came to it this time at some elemental level. My work at the Stanislavsky Theatre, where I'd been for several years, had come to an end, and to survive I had to make a complete break from *The Elder Daughter*. I'd started working on *King Lear* for the Moscow Arts, as well as something by Beckett, but for various reasons I'd been unable to go on with them. Yet the experience of thinking about these plays, as well as what was happening in my own life at the time, was leading me towards a totally new ideology of the theatre.

'Then there was Vampilov's *Duck-Shoot*, which I had rehearsed and worked on at the Theatre Institute. I suppose you might say I got my hand in with Vampilov. Directors have always been baffled by him – how to actually perform him, rather than merely reproduce his lines, or transfer him to the stage . . .

'In *The Elder Daughter* I found something that was both theatrical and psychological. *Serso* offers scope for the purely theatrical. Everything here is a game – the game of life itself, which the characters will either win or lose . . .'

Each of Vasilev's seven plays over the past ten years reaches out to the future, not through words or slogans but through people shaking off their chains. Each play is a brilliant theatrical game. The only thing which isn't a game for Vasilev is life itself. Everyone brave enough to follow him and his characters through to the bitter end will reach some profound, albeit painful reality within themselves, and will arrive at that final act which takes place off-stage, and which each of us must write for ourselves.

All of his productions are predicated on this final act. 'I see how split people are now,' he says. 'Yet their fundamental conflict isn't so much with the world as with themselves. It's not this person I'm putting on the stage but a certain creative moment, which involves destroying inner conflicts. I always say that the people of the future will be able to come and go and control the course of their own lives . . .'

Vasilev is one of those rare people whom Hermann Hesse called 'Men of Self-Will', who live by their own morality, their own inner laws. Society does not lightly forgive such people. Yet all of Vasilev's theatrical reverses have resulted in triumphs which owe nothing to the prevailing fashion.

'I call my theatre the primary school of drama,' he says, 'which strives to create a new world of its own in the theatre, just as Picasso or Leonardo created a new world in painting . . .'

It's hard to convey the feverish gleam in his eye, his unwaveringly steady nerve, and his capacity for work, which exhausts both himself and everyone around him; the autocratic demands he makes of his actors, and his humbleness before them; his utter dedication to the theatre, and his prostration at the start and end of a production, which is yet so charged with energy that not everyone can endure it.

People are constantly saying 'Are you ill, Tolya?' It's a question that infuriates him. Of course he's ill, permanently ill. But those actors who have been infected by the virus know what freedom is, for the exhausting road to his theatre will lead them to a knowledge of the truth, and having once embarked on it they will be unable ever again to lapse back into anaemic, castrated art.

'A good actor for me is a fellow-thinker, a comrade. In a play like *Serso*, for instance, this means someone who is standing at some sort of turning-point in his life, like the characters themselves . . .'

Serso is a play about my generation, about the people of the sixties who failed to nurture the first delicate buds of the thaw. What a lot we suffered with this play. First it was closed, then it opened again, but Vasilev has still not got his own permanent theatre in which to put it on.

'The grey people have arrived, the grey people have triumphed,' announces *Serso*. Meeting and parting, colliding and separating, grasping and releasing – Vasilev's scenes are constructed like a children's game. It's impossible to count how many of them there are, for none of the actors stands still for a second. It's as though they're coming to the end of a dance on which they embarked in their youth, and you don't immediately understand (for nothing in this play happens quickly) that they are merely circling on the spot, unable to stop.

Each of them dances to their own rhythm. Intimacy from a distance; proud independence, yet the almost morbid desire for a partner; the endless need to speak, yet the perpetual inability to do so; verbal debauchery, yet a prudish terror of words. All this twists and turns in endless scene changes whipped up by a cacophony of coloured lights, intensified by snatches of tunes from the characters' youth, suspended in the air by distant rolls of thunder and a piercing silence.

It's clear that we are meeting the characters at a point in their lives when one wrong step could be their downfall. They come on to the stage as strangers to one another, following a man named Petushok to the primordial peace of a boarded-up dacha outside Moscow. There, amidst the sounds of birdsong, they reach out to one another, hoping to find what they are looking for – a house, a husband, their lost youth.

As the play opens they are removing the boards from the dacha, letting in the light and air and releasing it and themselves from a long hibernation. This act of destruction and liberation suggests a settling of old scores, a fierce determination to put the wasted years behind them. But their liberation doesn't come quickly. In the play's last act (there are three, and it goes on for roughly four hours) we see them once again boarding up the house which has failed to give them refuge, for they sought salvation from outside, rather than within themselves.

As they hammer away, boarding up the house like a coffin, each blow seems to echo with impending death. 'I can't live like this! I'm shooting myself!' they say. Yet at the very moment when all has been said and they have reached rock bottom, they are liberated from their fears and their dependence on external events. Just when the coffin seems to be completely sealed up and everything appears to be over, we realise that it isn't the end at all, and we finally hear what they have been yearning all along to say to one another: 'I thought maybe now we could all live here together . . .'

'The play is indeed about people who are at a turning-point,' says Vasilev. 'Not because of something that has happened to them, but because they have reached the limits of their own existence – of normal everyday life, in other words. Events have played their part, of course. But there's no direct conflict, in the usual sense. Everyone has their own conflict with life and with themselves. This is the natural ebb and flow of life, which I learned to direct from watching the films of Fellini, especially *La Dolce Vita*. We all reach for the stars, but it's within us, that ebb and flow. Embedded in it are conflicts which become transformed during the course of the play. But at the end of *Serso* there's a break, and before stepping off into the unknown, they pause . . .

'The greatest problem for actors in a play like this is to be active, for there's no real activity as such in it. It means knowing how to move, a purely technical skill which nonetheless has taken over three years for them to learn. An even greater problem for them is that for the whole course of the play they have to be poets, standing on a stage above their lives . . .'

Victor Slavkin is now Vasilev's constant collaborator. The new kind of drama he represents shows us not life in the private mansions and spacious studies, but in the cramped tower-blocks and court-yards. His characters are revealed not at a moment of crisis, but in the process of examining their normal everyday lives. A lowly life and an elevated point of investigation: this is Vasilev's guiding principle as a director.

I once asked him if he would call his plays autobiographical. 'How can art *not* be autobiographical?' he retorted angrily. 'Each of my plays is the product of a certain stage of my life. And with each new play I start over again . . .'

Anatoly Vasilev isn't the only artist who was able to create when creativity itself seemed to be dead. But everyone experienced that era of despair in a different way. What seems unfair is that they weren't adults during the post-Stalin thaw, and that some of them became angry, others succumbed to despair, and still others to hysterical optimism or religious soul-searching.

For Vasilev the main thing was to search in the ruins for some scraps of freedom and dignity, whose discovery would inevitably bring him into conflict with his times. Yet this contradiction pro-vided the impulse to search yet further. Hence all his theoretical innovations, which help the actor to discover a dignified and liberat-ing existence for himself on the stage. Hence his impetuosity, his freedom, and his sense of play, so shockingly out of place in the dull and humourless seventies.

'I am so grateful to everyone who has travelled with me, to those who through choice or sheer chance left us, and to those who continue to make difficulties for us,' Vasilev says now. 'It is these people who have helped us to grow . . .'

And when he says that, we may be sure that it is no mere demonstration of the mysteries of the Russian soul, which is grim indeed when times are bad, and powerless when they are good.

Monument to a Witness
Vitaly Vitaliev

It is a sweltering day in August 1988, and although the era of stagnation is long past, the air is literally congealing in the damp Caucasus heat. A group of exhausted tourists meekly survey the panorama of the Novorossiisk cement works, read the slogan 'Cement Unites the Working Class!', and board their bus.

Our group has been so thoroughly cemented together by the heat that we don't immediately take in the strange building ahead which looks as if it's about to collapse. This iron and asphalt construction, at a 45 degree angle to the ground, is the memorial complex honouring those who died in the battles for the Small Earth region.*

The guide explains that it is supposed to symbolise the prow of a ship. Approaching this symbolic prow, we see on one of the symbolic sides of this symbolic ship a far from symbolic and very concrete gilded inscription, beneath which is a pleasantly familiar signature. 'Here you may read the words of Leonid Ilich Brezhnev, witness of the events at Small Earth,' says our guide, totally unaware of how new this honorary title of 'witness' is.

I remember visiting this memorial four years ago. The guide's words then were rather different, and went roughly as follows: 'On the right of this magnificent monument is an excerpt from the historic speech of our brilliant contemporary statesman and lieutenant, Leonid Ilich Brezhnev . . .'

Four years elapsed before the brilliant statesman could become an ordinary witness.

But he turned out not to be such an ordinary witness after all, as emerged later when our group entered the pleasantly cool and spacious womb of the symbolic ship. Here everything was suffused

* Area near Novorossiisk, on the Black Sea coast, which Soviet troops defended against the Nazis from February to September 1943.

with the 'brilliant statesman', starting with the granite bas-relief gallery of battle heroes. Everywhere there were quotes not of works he himself had written, but with his signature beneath them. One lengthy quote from a book entitled *Small Earth* was the background for a symbolic heart, alternately blazing up and sinking down under the glare of a searchlight. The excerpt was picked out in ribbon letters, intended to resemble the great leader's handwriting. Another quote from the same book – this time in gold letters – adorned the museum's exit.

I looked at this frankly tasteless heart – a particularly striking example of the sort of cheap kitsch which until recently has been so fashionable – and I thought . . . of the rights of authors. If everyone knows that *Small Earth* wasn't written by Brezhnev, his signature ought to be removed, and replaced by those of its authors.

I thought of the right of the organisers of this tawdry and pompous building to turn it into a monument to one man, even if he was a witness to the events on Small Earth.

And I thought finally of the right of memory. The memory of the hundreds of soldiers who fought for Small Earth, and of their commander, Tsezar Kunikov, who lost his life there. In its present form, the Small Earth complex represents a monument to the era of stagnation, when all our victories were attributed to one man, who was really nothing more than an ordinary witness.

Delay
Artak Chibukhyan

*A medical cyberneticist, born in Armenia
and living in Moscow, returns home.*

On the morning of 7 December I phoned home to Dilizhan, where I
was told that everyone was well. As soon as I put the phone down, the
earthquake started. I managed to get through again to Dilizhan and
learned that my family were all alive. Then the line was cut. That
afternoon I told my wife I was going to fly out there.

I realised it would be no good if volunteers simply poured into
Leninakan in a disorganised fashion, so I tried to discover where
doctors were being registered. But at our medical headquarters on
Kolpachny Street I was told that no more doctors were needed and I
should go under my own steam.

This was the first piece of stupidity I encountered, and it was just
as well I didn't believe them. I'd seen just three seconds of the
devastation on the television news, and those three seconds were
enough to give me some idea of what things were really like out there.
I also realised that it would be virtually impossible to get enough
doctors into the town in two days. I was soon to discover just how
desperately needed we were.

The following evening I threw a raincoat over my suit, grabbed a
spare pair of socks, and met up with the rest of our group at
Moscow's Vnukovo airport. By 4 a.m. on 9 December we were in
Yerevan. Dawn was breaking as we boarded a small Yak-40 plane
crammed with passengers bound for Leninakan. People on the plane
spoke of nothing but the tragedy there, and as someone completely
outside the political struggle I must say that on that day I heard not
one word about the riots in Nagorno-Karabakh. I shall never forget
that.

We drove from the airport to what remained of Leninakan's First

Hospital. One of the buildings was still intact, manned by medical students from Voronezh and Volgograd. Amputated limbs were being dumped in an upstairs room and the students asked me to help, so I piled up the limbs and got some soldiers to burn them. Then we listed the names of everyone in our group, and what our specialities were, and said we were prepared to do anything. One of us took this list off to the town's medical headquarters, and soon returned saying 'They told us to do whatever we wanted!'

I went out on to the street, and a man in a car with a two-way radio drew up, asked me if I was a doctor, and told me to jump in. He drove me to a first-aid station. 'Here's a doctor for you,' he told them. This man turned out to be the director of the Surdzhyan medical institute. I later discovered that his pregnant wife had been buried beneath the ruins of the maternity home, but that he had stayed working at his post.

The chief doctor at the first-aid station, Dr Torosyan, who was also working round the clock, took us off to a first-aid ambulance and said 'Drive!' And although I told him I was a medical cyberneticist, I soon realised that I would be working here as a nurse or nursing auxiliary if need be.

I joined a team bound for the city centre. I knew that Leninakan had once been the most beautiful town in Armenia, but I had never seen it before. I saw that dead town then, though, and we doctors must have witnessed the tragedy as few others did, for people tell us the things that are too painful to tell anyone else.

No one who came to Leninakan could hold back the tears. Things were very, very hard. Everyone was summoning up their last drop of strength to help.

But first-aid work teaches you a lot, and I returned to Moscow with a feeling of despondency that was far more oppressive than the exhaustion of the past few days. I went to talk to the editors of the magazine *Motherland*, but they suggested that I write up my experiences and bring them in. This didn't interest me. I wanted someone to ask me about how things had been organised. And this is what I would have told them.

There seemed to me to be enough doctors at the hospital, but at the first-aid centre they were in desperately short supply. Who was responsible for saying that Leninakan had enough doctors? And where was the network of hospitals they kept telling us about before we left Moscow?

Instead I saw people being dragged from the debris by volunteers, organised in teams of five. As non-professionals, they had to learn as they went along, at the price of human lives . . .

There are some basic rules for rescuing people trapped under the rubble of destroyed buildings. The medical phenomenon known as 'crush syndrome' was first observed during the bombing of London in the last war. If you don't apply a tourniquet to crushed extremities before pulling a person out, they may die. Any doctor will tell you this. But when an untrained volunteer heaves away at a joist which has fallen on top of someone, they can't be expected to know that they're likely to kill the person they're struggling so hard to save.

Once, as we returned from the airport to collect a patient, we saw a man dancing about on the road and waving to us. 'We've just found my nephew alive! It's a miracle! I thought I'd lost my whole family, but my nephew's alive! I heard his voice! They're lifting up that paving-stone now and getting him out!'

We waited for them to drag away the paving-stone, but we already knew the worst. Rigor mortis had already set in, and the man who had just heard the voice of his beloved nephew broke down like a child and became virtually incoherent.

Once when we were working in the rubble a paving-stone rocked and breathed, and there was a trickle of sand. Artur Arutyunyan, who was the thinnest, managed to get through to a little boy. He gave him an injection, and we gave him the kiss of life. He died twice as we were taking him to the airport, and twice we managed to resuscitate him, using nail-scissors instead of scalpels. Finally, on the helicopter, the child died.

That evening we rescued another survivor. He stopped breathing, and we resuscitated him. He died again, and again we resuscitated him, and when at last we got him to the hospital they said: 'You've brought us a corpse.'

'But he was breathing a moment ago!' we said.

I massaged his heart, gave him mouth-to-mouth resuscitation and put him in an oxygen tent, and he started breathing. Next day he was dead.

The first professional rescue parties arrived in Leninakan on about 10 December. At least it was on the 10th that I heard of the arrival of a mountain rescue team from Karaganda, although I only actually saw them on the 15th. Some volunteers had just cleared away the rubble to reveal a woman survivor. Completely baffled as to what to do next, they phoned through to the Karaganda team. I happened to be with a member of this team, and heard him shouting down the phone at the volunteers. There were sixty-eight people all working on the same spot, he said; volunteers should be organised into groups, each headed by a professional.

But for this kind of leadership structure, some sort of two-way communication is needed. I saw no sign of this in Leninakan, and on 9 and 10 December there was no leadership at all to speak of. There were virtually no first-aid ambulances in the town immediately after the tragedy. Yet from the moment the earthquake struck until 15 December, there was a flood of survivors urgently needing to be put on planes and flown to hospitals. At least fifty ambulances were needed – assuming that the roads were clear for fast traffic, and that there was a soldier or policeman on every street corner with a two-way radio.

As it was, the streets were crammed with a pitifully inadequate number of ambulances forcing their way through the crowds to the airport and back. We simply cruised around the town, helping whoever stopped us first. The cost of this can be measured in human lives. There was no other cost in Leninakan then.

Sometimes it took us literally three hours to ferry a patient from the town to the airport. One of our team would have to get out of the car, walk on ahead, and get the other cars out of the way. Then, having pushed and shoved our way on to a plane, we would return for another patient, who might well have died before we got to them. This would go on round the clock. In twenty-four hours one car could get eight patients to hospital. But there weren't enough ambulances. Later ten arrived from Georgia, for which many thanks . . .

As for drugs, there wasn't enough hydrogen peroxide, there were no pain-killers at all apart from aspirin, and I didn't see any imported drugs until the 12th and 13th. There were no experienced pharmacists, or indeed pharmacists of any kind, and priceless drugs were distributed at the airport by students, who would just open Makhaevsky's standard reference book when they had a spare moment and look up the international name of this or that drug.

Such a lot of people helped or tried to help. The French medical teams were the first on the scene. A French team brought a woman patient to us at the airport. Her wounds were freshly dressed, she had all the drugs she needed, and she was wrapped up in a special sheet brought by an Israeli team, one side of which keeps the body warm, and the other side cool.

I also met a doctor from Komi. A group of them had flown out on the 8th or 9th with cranes, first-aid teams, doctors, and medical supplies. They were splendidly equipped and worked beautifully, and many, many thanks to them.

Then there was a team of students from Moscow's First Medical Institute who set up a chemist's in a tent on the main square, and when one of them had a moment they would take a bag and go around the town from tent to tent. These students found exactly the right way to help, and when new first-aid teams arrived they would join them. They were wonderful kids.

But how many doctors were sitting around doing nothing! I saw no special emergency routine in the hospital during those crucial first few days. All that came later. But I shall never forget the initial delays.

Our medical services operate badly even in non-emergencies. Everyone knows this, and our child mortality rate is one of the most terrible proofs of it.

It would be naïve to imagine that things would simply start to run smoothly in a crisis. Yet people did indeed imagine just that. We need instead to work out an orderly emergency routine which can go into action at a moment's notice. We have no such routine. What we have instead is mass voluntary mobilisation.

Before the earthquake, Leninakan was under curfew. After it the curfew was the lifted. At first this seemed like a humane move: people in a state of grief couldn't tear themselves away from the ruins of their homes, feeling that they had to do something. Yet was it really so humane when their clumsy efforts cost us so many lives?

I begged, pleaded, and shouted at people to get away and stop obstructing our work, raising dust, and shifting the debris. Day after day, precious time was lost moving back crowds of people and cars.

Why did looters appear in the town? Why weren't people moved away from their destroyed homes? Why did they kill their loved ones through sheer ignorance of the most elementary rules of life-saving? Why did apathy and passivity take over? Why were bodies allowed to lie out on the streets?

For five whole days I didn't wash my hands. Later some special emulsion arrived. Lots of things arrived later. Almost everything we needed, in fact. But we didn't have these things at the beginning, and we paid a heavy price for this delay. Too many people died who might have been ferried out and resuscitated.

This was the price of the delay and of the misdirected 'kindness' which prevented us from taking the necessary measures. These measures were first laid down by Dr Pirogov over a hundred years ago – during the Crimean War!

First of all, martial law should have been introduced at once; I'm sure that people would have understood the need for it. Secondly, the scientific military-medical rules governing these disasters should have been applied. All the remaining details which hampered our work, and sometimes threatened the risk of an epidemic, were of secondary importance and would never have arisen if strict discipline had been maintained in the town.

I know that martial law invariably leads to economic decline and collapse . . . in the end. But not initially. To begin with there's always a leap forward. Within two or three weeks, say, martial law can control a situation which is close to panic and halt the spread of chaos and disorganisation. In practice this means clearing crowds of people and cars off the streets, which will then be free for ambulances and first-aid vehicles. It means faster communication and more efficiently controlled supplies. It means the proper organisation of rescue work.

Any military doctor's manual will mention the need for field kitchens. Field kitchens appeared only on the seventh day. On the sixth, people started clearing away the filth, and first-aid doctors started on their own authority to give rescue workers prolonged-action antibiotics. Martial law would have ensured that all this was planned properly in advance.

I also saw no proper evacuation procedure in operation until the fifth day. I don't know if the local authorities panicked. I know ordinary people worked desperately hard and went for days without sleep. But ordinary people unfortunately don't know the rules of organised rescue work. If they don't know these rules and civil defence is simply a fiction, then we must get rid of the people who have been in charge of it and start afresh.

From 13 December, we first-aid doctors were asking for vascular-dilating drugs to prevent brain clots.

'Why do you need them?' we were asked.

'Because people may start having strokes and heart attacks.'

'Really . . . ?'

We collected extra supplies of bandages, because we realised that people would soon start coming to us with festering sores that hadn't previously been attended to. We were doing the work of military paramedics. But even a paramedic carrying out his duties on the battlefield couldn't imagine what things were like in Leninakan then. A paramedic wouldn't have had to work out all the foreign names of the various drugs, and what kind of syringe was needed. Doctors shouldn't have to be thinking about such things either.

The sort of medical supplies needed on this sort of massive scale is another, even more painful issue. I have simply tried to describe the most important things as I saw them, and to demand that the delays be fully investigated. Possibly with the full severity of the law.

Since returning from Armenia I have lost all enthusiasm for my work. I hope it will return. The moment my doctor friends got back to Moscow, we met to discuss our experiences, and decided to make the following proposal to the Soviets of Ministers of the USSR and the republics: that they create an organisation of emergency doctors, who could go at any moment to the disaster area and give properly qualified help, and could hold annual meetings up and down the country at which they could improve their skills.

Recent tragic events in Georgia prove how urgently needed this is. And even more recent events in Tadjikistan demand it.

Letter to the Jury of the Miss Charm 1989 Contest

Dear Comrades,

I don't know if I'm going about this the right way, but I'm writing to you anyway. So far as I can see from a short television report, the forthcoming international Miss Charm 1989 contest has persuaded a large number of well-known people to sit on its jury.

From the sublime to the ridiculous is but a short step, but between charm and beauty stands an ocean. Beauty is defined by rules and norms and can be easily assessed by measuring bust, hips, and so on, whereas charm is a God-given gift which cannot possibly be measured.

I'm sure quite a few men share this view, so come off it, all you respected men, why on earth have you agreed to take part in these ludicrous proceedings? You must know that, whilst charm has no price, beauty has to be paid for. And pay for it they have, since it costs twenty-five roubles to enter the contest, and that money doesn't come out of thin air!

> Masha Dmitrieva, seventeen-year-old Moscow
> schoolgirl

The Children of the Basements
Vitaly Eryomin

One in eight of all teenagers sent to juvenile work camps are there for sexual assaults and rape. And since most sexual crimes are either not reported to the police or thrown out by the courts, the true number is far higher.

Until recently the whole issue was a 'forbidden' topic. Now at last we can admit that we won't make the problem go away merely by shutting our eyes to it.

I

It is 10 a.m. on 2 January at the 39th precinct of Moscow's Perovsky district police station, where I am waiting to see the inspector for juvenile offenders. In the next room a young lieutenant is talking to a young girl, brought in for drinking vodka. 'It's bad for you. Your brain's not fully developed. And perestroika means that you can be held responsible . . .' The girl rolls her eyes with boredom.

The inspector finally appears, and I ask her the address of the basements in the area where young people get together.

'Number 3 and number 12 Vladimirskaya Street,' she says.

'Is that all?' I ask.

'Yes,' she replies.

I find this hard to believe. There are literally thousands of basements and bomb-shelters throughout Moscow, to which teenagers go to drink alcohol, sniff glue, and take drugs. Vagrants hide out in them and lure young people into their squalid underground existence. And people get murdered there.

The father of a teenage girl sexually assaulted in one of these basements recently encountered a similar lack of interest from the 39th precinct, and decided to come to *Ogonyok* with his story instead.

'On 7 November last year I came home from celebrating Revolution Day with friends,' he told me, 'and when I looked into Tanya's room I saw her sobbing her heart out, with a bruise under her left eye.'

Tanya's friend, seventeen-year-old Inna, took up the story:

'We'd gone to the Glory cinema to see *Curse of the Valley of Snakes*, and four lads came up. Two were about seventeen, that's Chuck and Khaba, and the other two, Bullock and Boss, were about fifteen.

' "Sell your tickets and let's go for a walk instead," they said. We didn't want to, so we lent them forty kopecks to buy tickets, and we all went into the film together. Afterwards they asked us again to go for a walk and see their basement where they did weight-lifting.

'Like idiots, we agree. Chuck and Khaba look all right, and Bullock and Boss are just a couple of kids. Boss rips off a flag from the cinema foyer and starts waving it around, but Chuck tells him to cut it out. Then Khaba disappears and comes back with two bottles of booze. Let's celebrate the revolution and our friendship, he says. I take a swig, but Tanya doesn't want any.

'Then they take us down to their basement. There's no weight-lifting equipment, just a little room with an iron door and an old sofa. They take Tanya in there, and Chuck stops me, saying: "Now look here, we didn't bring you here to show you our weight-lifting, but to rape you."

' "No girl's got away from us yet!" Khaba says. "Just you try telling on us! It won't do you any good!"

'Just then someone living in the building came down to the basement, and we managed to escape . . .'

'Something had to be done,' said Tanya's father. 'We had to find and punish the bastards. Khaba and his gang had to be put out of action before other girls visited that basement. But Tanya was too terrified to give their names, let alone identify them.

'She finally gave in, though, and I got on the phone to the inspector for juvenile offenders at the 39th precinct.

' "Where was the basement?" she asked.

' "The girls have forgotten. They cut through the courtyards."

' "Well, we know where it is anyway."

'I thought she would ask me what the rapists looked like, but instead she wanted to know Tanya's surname, and why the girls had gone there in the first place. There was a clear presumption of guilt in her voice! I imagined my daughter being subjected to this sort of questioning during the investigation, and told the inspector I wasn't giving my name, but wanted to be sure that she had a record of my statement.

'"You're being so vague!" said the inspector.

'"But I have to be. My daughter's life is at risk."

'"So what? Our lives are at risk every day!"

'I gritted my teeth and hung up with the clear impression she wouldn't lift a finger to help us. I was on my own . . .'

Tanya's father eventually managed to discover the technical college where Khaba was a student, and he took the opportunity to talk to the director, the deputy director, and Khaba's work-group leader about the sort of moral guidance their students got.

'You can't make a silk purse out of a sow's ear,' said the director. 'These kids aren't interested in anything. We organise discussions on the danger of drugs and alcohol, and generally try to instil a bit of decency into them . . .'

The group leader added: 'We discuss specific cases relating to Articles 206, 117, and 145 of the Criminal Code, on rape, robbery, and hooliganism, and we give them the names of the people involved and the length of their prison sentences. That gives them something to think about.'

'Someone from the criminal investigation department is attached to each course,' chipped in the deputy director. 'Not a day passes when we don't have some judge or inspector here from the 39th precinct. We even have a competition on the law, and someone from the police department gives them marks!'

So how would the director get Khaba to see the error of his ways?

'I'd say to him: "Stop sponging off the state and get on with your work! They used to shoot people like you during the Civil War, and a good thing too!"'

2

For every rapist there is a victim. Our society must now contain a fair number of women who have been raped as teenagers and have concealed it from their parents. What sort of wives and mothers will these women make?

Over the past year the 39th precinct has investigated six juvenile attempted rape cases, and in only one of these was the crime actually proved and the guilty tried. The explanation for this is only too obvious.

'When questioning a rape victim, it is important to record her account in a way that is neither sketchy nor dull. Her emotional experiences should be reflected as accurately as possible, and the interviewer should help her to formulate her story thoroughly and clearly, ensuring that no detail is omitted . . .'

These admirable sentiments are contained in a guidebook for investigators as they negotiate their way through the contradictions between the evidence of the victim and her attackers.

Yet many rapes take extremely perverted and sadistic forms, and the investigator generally has an enormous case-load to attend to. He will ask the girl endless questions in a bored, weary voice, and inform her that she will face a medical examination, a face-to-face confrontation with her attackers, and finally a trial, with all its inevitable attendant publicity. The last thing the poor girl wants is to have to tell this stranger what she was made to do, let alone 'thoroughly and clearly'.

If a teenage girl gets into trouble, the consequences will be emotionally agonising for her; the trial will bring shame upon her, and her parents may consider her guilt greater than that of those who raped her.

So it's hardly surprising that so many rapes go unreported, or are reported only days later, by which time crucial pieces of evidence may have been lost. Since many rapists operate in gangs, they may invent a mass of fictitious alibis, and group pressure may be put on the investigation, the trial, the girl's parents, and the girl herself. Even if criminal proceedings do go ahead, the criminals don't necessarily get their come-uppance, and it's quite common for rapists to demand money from their victim, threatening to broadcast her disgrace to the world if she doesn't comply.

I wonder what would happen if we *did* discover the true extent of rapes and sexual assaults, or how many under-age girls are registered at VD clinics, or have abortions, or hang about in railway stations, basements, and secret hide-outs. What would all this teenage sexual delinquency show us, apart from confirming the extent of the disorders in our schools, our colleges, and our families? What would it tell us about parents who know no other way of bringing up their children than to hit them? Or teachers incapable of instilling the most elementary decency into their pupils?

Rapists don't appear from nowhere. They themselves are the children of violence.

Conversation with My Son
Yury Paporov

I have been reading our periodical press for many decades now, yet I had never noticed. Or rather I couldn't *not* notice, but I never stopped to think about it.

Until yesterday. I was reading this year's first issue of the magazine *Village Youth*, and my eye was caught by the familiar logo on the bottom of the inside cover: 'Proletarians of the World, Unite!'

My eleven-year-old son, seeing me staring at it, leaned over and asked: 'Who are these proletarians, Dad?' I started to explain, but this brought up yet more questions.

Luckily I was saved at this point by a ring at the doorbell, and my son's friend dragged him off for a walk.

Next morning I set aside everything else and set off for the periodical room of the Lenin Library, where I discovered that the overwhelming majority of Soviet journals and newspapers open with the slogan. Even magazines such as *Stud Farming and Equestrian Sport*, *Beekeeping*, *Cement*, *Tractors and Farm Machines*, *Pipeline Construction*, *Welding in Industry*, and *How to Serve Your Community*. A whole range of magazines, however, including *Soviet Union*, *Soviet Screen*, *Soviet Stage and Circus*, and *The Individual and the Law*, do without it.

Unfortunately none of this helped me to answer my son's question. Indeed, it only confused matters, since several journals published in Russian, and read by no one but Sovietologists and Soviet citizens, carry the call, but it is missing from publications specifically *addressed* to the world proletariat, such as *Soviet Union*, *Soviet Woman*, *New Times*, *Foreign Trade*, *History of the USSR*, and *Peoples of Asia and Africa*.

'Proletarians of the World, Unite!' Deriving from Marx and Engels, this was adopted in 1847 as the slogan of the Union of Communists, it crowns the text of the Communist Manifesto, and is the slogan of the Soviet Communist Party and the international Communist movement. Its meaning is clear to all, a short utterance, providing a guide to thought and action.

So far, so good. And yet . . . Why is its use so inconsistent, so unsystematic, and so unintelligent? Why must we turn slogans into mere ornaments? And how was I to explain the whole thing to my son in such a way that he wouldn't get into trouble at school?

I returned from the Lenin Library with no clear answers for my son, and I await answers from other *Ogonyok* readers better informed than I.

Condemned to Solitude: A Conversation with Alfred Schnittke
Anna Kagarlitskaya

The composer of numerous symphonic, chamber, choral, and instrumental works, as well as ballet, theatre, and film scores, Alfred Schnittke is a member of the Swedish, Bavarian, and East and West Berlin academies of arts, and is widely regarded in the West as one of the most important musicians in the world today. Yet his own country has failed to do him justice for most of his working life.

Schnittke is one of a whole generation of musicians of the 1950s, among them Sofia Gubaidulina, Edison Denisov, and Arvo Pärt. His works include an extraordinary range of styles, genres, periods, and cultures, whose result is a model of polysemantic power yet is accessible to even the most musically unsophisticated audiences. People are often amazed to discover in it some revelation about pain and joy, the eternal and the fleeting. But grand words are out of place here, for the music is as modest, dignified, and free of rhetoric as the composer himself.

I met him in his three-room flat in Moscow's Dmitrii Ulyanov Street, surrounded by scores, tapes, records, and a Petrof piano, and I asked what had started his interest in composing.

'Before the war I lived with my grandparents in Moscow. They put me in for the entrance exam for the Central Music School, but I can't even remember if I passed or not. When war broke out I was sent back to my parents in Engels, where I lived until 1946. After the war, we got back our confiscated wireless sets, and I started listening to music – I especially liked operatic arias, and longed to sing. I remember listening to the first performance of Shostakovich's Ninth Symphony at that time, but it didn't make much impression on me. I had no other contact with music – apart from a couple of times I got my hands on a mouth-organ our neighbour had picked up off a German soldier in the war.

'My father was of German origin, and when I was twelve we moved to Vienna, where he worked as a translator for the German-language paper *Österreichische Zeitung*. He was once awarded a Höhner accordion by his employers. It had all the bass notes missing, but I managed to compose a tune on it, after which I was taken to the top floor of our building, where a woman named Frau Ruber started giving me piano lessons. I soon started composing things – a concerto for accordion and orchestra, followed by some piano preludes. I even wrote a piece which contained two themes, and I was amazed when Frau Ruber said it was in sonata form!

'After two years in Vienna we came home and settled in a village called Valentinovka, just outside Moscow.

'In August 1949, just before the start of the new school year, a man came to visit our neighbours who was the accountant at Moscow's October Revolution music school, and he persuaded me to apply. I went along with my father and played the examiners something on the piano – very badly; I revealed my complete ignorance of musical theory, and did a test which showed that I lacked perfect pitch. I did have very good relative pitch, however, and I was accepted in the choral conducting department, where none of this mattered so much. Not long afterwards I started studying theory with Iosif Ryzhkin. It was to him that I showed my first semi-professional compositions, and he took me along to the Conservatoire, where I entered Evegeny Golubev's composition class.

'My musical life progressed quite smoothly after that. But I often wonder how things would have turned out if that accountant hadn't turned up . . .'

I asked Schnittke if he felt that music was getting lost amidst the current maelstrom in our cultural life.

'I think music faces as many problems and contradictions as every other aspect of our life today. What we have seen recently, though, is a somewhat inordinate emphasis on rock music, which after being suppressed for so long has temporarily ousted everything else.

'There has always been this passion for modernity. A hundred years ago the Viennese waltz was to music rather what rock music is today. Then in the twenties we had the jazz era, and jazz seemed to push out everything else. But in fact it did no such thing, and I don't think it will happen now. What will happen is what always happens: more and more musical genres will appear, music's boundaries will widen, contemporary classical music will develop, and the wave of rock music will eventually subside, as it's already doing in the West. I'm actually extremely interested in rock, and follow its development very closely. What I am against is the mindless capitulation to the first thing that comes along, be it rock music or anything else.'

A number of serious Soviet composers are now pursuing a synthesis of styles, often closer to 'light' music. Did this so-called 'third direction' appeal to Schnittke?

'This notion of a "third direction" is nothing new, of course. When Gershwin broke the rules of conventional opera in the thirties with *Porgy and Bess*, it was regarded as something totally new. Then there was Stravinsky. Or take Satie, who even before the First World War was writing all sorts of musical parodies and satires.

'Nowadays we are far too quick to distinguish between different kinds of music. Yet even the most conventional distinction between "light" and "serious" music must contain a momentary acknowledgement of something utterly private and transcendental. Time sums up all the parts, and the future, which remains unknown to us, will receive the whole picture of the world we now inhabit.

'This has always been so. In the twelfth century, there were two totally different kinds of music: the songs of the Minnesingers and a newly emerging professional music. Whereas today we no longer make such distinctions, of course, but see both as part of the same musical world.

'Or take Bach. His English or French suites might have struck some people then as "light" in comparison with his masses. But a hundred years later such distinctions were irrelevant, and both tendencies were seen as an integral part of Bach's musical universe. So I am sure the time will come when modern musical trends no longer seem "modern" at all.

'Yet our existence is certainly constructed on both a lower and a higher level, and people live on both levels simultaneously, not because they're unprincipled, but because these polarities are inherent in life itself.

'When I wrote my First Symphony in 1972 I was trying to reveal the interaction between the two levels. I spent four years writing this symphony, and in it I tried to express everything I felt about the symphonic form and the technology of music.

'It consists of several different layers – a serious language as well as a quasi-serious one, made up of quotes from the finest examples of world music, such as Beethoven's Fifth Symphony, Tchaikovsky's First Piano Concerto, and Chopin's Funeral March. I introduced these into my symphony in a distorted form – by which I mean vulgarised through frequent repetition. You can transform any true idea into a lie simply by repeating it over and over again, like a sort of happiness pill. This is what has happened to all the "popular classics" we hear endlessly on the radio.

'My symphony also contains another layer, consisting of quotes and pseudo-quotes from music I wrote for various films – innumerable walzes and brass band marches written to directors' orders. There are other quotes too: Gregorian chant, jazz, even fascist marches. All of these elements constantly interact, like a game, and the work opens with the musicians running on stage playing their instruments.

'Its first performance was in the town of Gorky, conducted by Gennady Rozhdestvensky, and its second was in 1975 in Tallinn, conducted by Eri Klas. It provoked a storm of publicity, and for the next ten years it wasn't performed at all. Then a few years ago the director of the Hamburg ballet, John Neumeyer, used it as the music for his ballet *A Streetcar Named Desire*.'

I asked if Schnittke could describe the role his generation of musicians had played in the development of modern Soviet music.

'From 1953 onwards there was a steady revival of interest in new musical developments. In that year Shostakovich's Tenth Symphony was performed for the first time since 1948 – this had been the low point in the history of Soviet music, when the authorities issued their decree banning Muradeli's opera *The Great Friendship*. Shostakovich's symphony had an immense impact on everyone – the majority, who took up arms against it, the minority, who liked and supported it, and all those in the middle who didn't know what they were supposed to feel about it. In those days people still couldn't say what they thought, not so much because they were afraid (although some still were), but because they no longer trusted their own judgement.

'Things moved very fast after that. In 1953 we still had to get a special pass at the recording room of the Moscow Conservatoire to listen to tapes of Stravinsky and Bartok – let alone Schoenberg. But by 1955 we could listen to all of them quite freely. Everything that had been forbidden in 1948 was given back to us, and until about 1961 banished works were constantly being resurrected.

'Then in 1962 Edison Denisov and various other composers began to attend the annual Warsaw festival of contemporary music, from which they would bring back tapes of the latest works of Penderecki, Berio, and Nono. All this broadened our musical horizons, and in 1963 Luigi Nono visited our country and performed some of his works before the Union of Composers. It was a revelation to us. We had been told that avant-garde composers were all dry, alien machine-men. But Nono wasn't like that, he was sensitive, impulsive, and temperamental. Soon after this we started listening to the works of other composers, such as Stockhausen, Lutoslawski, and Ligeti, and exchanging scores, books, and records with them.

'In the late 1960s I realised that I wanted to teach others, but that I would also have to be alone if I was to avoid merely chronicling the latest fashions.

'It was then that I started working in the film industry. This set me very specific and often not very demanding tasks, which had to be reconciled with my musical ambitions outside film. I had to produce film scores which weren't mere hack work, while establishing my own unique personal centre from which to write music that was life-enhancing, not mere lifeless avant-gardism. I know there is no single recipe for this, and that we are all condemned to solitude, but I continue searching nonetheless.

'1968 was a time of colossal enthusiasm. Although no one could make sense of it at the time, I am now convinced that everyone alive on earth then was experiencing something. It was in that year that Stockhausen's *Seven Days* appeared, a sort of musical meditation, written not in notes but in words. Music seemed to be moving on to a wholly new plane, ruled more by words than by pure musical technique. We thought then that some mighty convulsion lay ahead which would propel us on to yet another plane of thought, intuition, and God knows what else.

'But it didn't happen. For artists in other countries, 1968 was a time of powerful subjective impressions. For us it was the start of an era of stagnation, and instead of attaining that higher level of reality where everything fits and there's an explanation for everything, these changes merely continued to be reflected in our own personal lives.

'It was in 1968 that I wrote the music for Andrei Kzhizhanovsky's animated fable *The Glass Accordion*, about the devaluation of morality, the invasion of the bureaucracy, and the crisis in our culture. This film upset the film authorities quite a bit, and until recently enjoyed a semi-underground status. My music for it includes all sorts of styles and themes, quotes and pseudo-quotes. But the high point in my understanding of that period came with my First Symphony, in 1972. Never before or since did I attempt to be so open and undogmatic.

'I also wrote several articles about the music of Shostakovich, Prokofiev, and Stravinsky. Stravinsky has been much maligned recently for jumping about from one style to another. But when comparing such very different works as *The Rite of Spring*, *A Soldier's Tale*, *Ragtime*, *Kiss of the Fairy*, and *Requiem*, I saw that however much he jumped about, he always remained Stravinsky. All these works merely express a different aspect of his personality. He was a child of his time – not simply following the latest fashion, but bearing witness to and finding musical expression for the ever-accelerating pace of life then.

'And as for the accelerated pace of our lives today . . . ! One has only to switch on the wireless and wander over the airwaves to embrace a vast world of sound. I've come to feel that one shouldn't resist this but should relate to it as a fact of modern life. The problem is how to hang on to one's individuality within this vast world of polystylism.'

Schnittke's music has had an enormous influence on our cinema. He has written scores for some of the finest Soviet films of the past twenty years, including *Commissar*, *Morning Stars*, *The 6th of July*, *Uncle Vanya*, *Agony*, *Ascent*, and *The Little Tragedies*. He brings to film his understanding of the world, and film breathes new life into the rather self-enclosed world of his work.

'I haven't worked in the film industry for several years, because it didn't leave me enough time for my own work. Unfortunately my whole attitude to films is determined by the need to earn money. Teaching at the Conservatoire brought in almost nothing, and between 1962 and 1978 several things I wrote were performed in public, but nothing was bought by the Ministry of Culture or the radio. So in the end I just had to make a living.

'But even so I always tried to get as much as I could out of film work. My first picture was Igor Talankin's *Entrance*, and I worked with Talankin for many years. I went on to work with Elem Klimov, Larissa Shchepitko, Alexander Mitta, Andrei Kzhizhanovsky, Andrei Smirnov, and Mikhail Schweitzer. These people have been very important for me, often more for who they are. Smirnov's *Byelorussian Station*, for instance, simply couldn't bear the weight of a full score, and we finally settled for an orchestration of a Bulat Okudjava song. In another of Smirnov's films, *Autumn*, I was unhappy with my efforts to reproduce a rock music style.'

When *Autumn* was made, rock was still deeply underground, and that was the basis of its popularity. I asked Schnittke if rock wouldn't inevitably lose its poignancy now that it is out in the open.

'Yes. And many writers and artists who have long derived their authority from a halo of repression also suddenly seem rather insubstantial now that they can speak out freely. Bulgakov, Pasternak, Mandelstam, Akhmatova, and Tsvetaeva are still as marvellous as ever, of course. And writers like Aitmatov, Voznesensky, Bitov, and Granin offer our literature a lot of hope. But there was also a feeling that something sensationally new might appear, and it hasn't. You have to have something to say, not merely know how to say it.'

Is this a problem Schnittke has faced?

'Not really. Like many of my colleagues, I've always done what I felt I had to do, regardless of circumstances. Things are always changing anyway – one minute they're against you, and at present they seem to be all for us. Which doesn't mean that this recent interest in my work may not suddenly evaporate. But I can't endlessly adapt to suit changing interests. I work out of some inner need and now, thank God, this need is in tune with the prevailing climate.

'Almost three years ago I had a major heart attack, and it now seems as though as much has happened to me in these last three years as in the previous ten. My subjective time is much more in tune with historic time. I used to be endlessly meeting people, going to concerts and the theatre, and it all seemed terribly important. Then I had to take a month off, and when I came back I realised that nothing terrible had happened because I didn't talk to so-and-so, or go to a concert. I realised that I could live without it, but had just never had the strength to admit it.

'Now it has all dropped away of itself, and I almost never leave the house. I don't know what tomorrow will bring, only that tomorrow I shall be sitting down to work as usual from eleven to one, and from five to seven . . .'

Exhibition of Achievements
Yury Belyavsky and Vitaly Vitaliev

When visiting the Exhibition of Economic Achievements of the USSR one is invariably reminded of Gorky's sad words: 'Humble truths are more precious than the ennobling lie.' These 'humble truths' turn to dust before the exhibition's monumental arch, whose latticed gates resemble those of the Winter Palace . . .

The Exhibition of Economic Achievements is not only a town within a town, but a state within a state. A miniature model of our vast country with all its existing features intact: its own Soviet of Ministers, masquerading as a board of directors; its own ministry pavilions; its own draughty minibuses, popularly known as 'barefoot riders'; even its own police force.

It isn't simply a model, it's a symbol of our great country, covering an area of 750 acres. A symbol 'exalting' us to the shining heights, where cramped communal flats and squalid five-storey prefabs are transformed into splendid sculpted palaces; where instead of queues for dirty-pink sausage which you wouldn't give to the cat, we see a rich abundance of veal and sturgeon; and where antediluvian educational machines are replaced by gleaming electronic miracles of scientific and technological progress – of strictly limited availability, of course.

How sweet it used to be to wander around this fantasy world, blissfully murmuring to oneself: 'We *can* do it if we try . . .'

We never used to doubt the ennobling power of this lie, never paused to think that all lies degrade us, liers and lied-to alike . . .

It is a fine Saturday, and we are trudging along the exhibition's deserted main alley. The crunch of our footsteps on the untrodden crust of snow harmonises with the rousing music blaring from the ubiquitous loudspeakers. The music merely intensifies the general atmosphere of gloom. Frozen on either side of the alley are pompous turreted pavilions, in the Stalinist Gothic style, as though congealed by the frost.

Where are the visitors, an average of 30,000 a day? Where are the rosy-cheeked crowds of Muscovites and Soviet tourists, pouring into what the guidebooks describe as 'this astonishing world of science and technology, our national university and one of Moscow's most popular spots'?

Maybe they are hiding in the pavilions. Let us find out.

Here is the Cosmos pavilion. In the vast, freezing exhibit-filled hangar we count eight visitors. Here, we have been told, there is meant to be an exhibition of recent discoveries. But the door leading to the exhibition is bolted shut, and guarded by two old women in fur coats.

'The exhibition's closed!' they chorus.

'We can see that,' we say.

'Well, it's closed and it isn't closed. You have to have a pass,' they say.

'A closed exhibition,' we muse in astonishment. 'What an odd notion!'

'*We* don't know,' reply the women. 'They just told us not to let anyone in without a special pass . . . We can see you're all right, but we still can't let you in . . .'

We didn't meet one visitor in the Electrification of the USSR pavilion, or in Soviet Trade Unions or Popular Education, and the steps of the barred and bolted pavilion of the Meat and Milk Industry were covered in three feet of virgin snow. Clearly no one had come this way for a very long time – although we did manage to get inside the following day, and could gaze to our hearts' content at the mountains of wonderful sausages and tinned delicacies.

In our search for something open, we stumbled across yet another 'closed' exhibition with a long and beautiful name – Unremitting Attention to the Production of Foodstuffs. 'Entrance by Permit Only' read the angry sign adorning the doors of Pavilion no. 1, where the exhibition was being held. Passes were evidently an essential precondition of this 'unremitting attention' to the production of foodstuffs. Our journalistic credentials were carefully checked by a young man with a two-way radio, who graciously admitted us to the exhibition, yelling after us: 'No photographs!'

What we saw was worthy of an artist's palette: all fifteen republics of the Soviet Union, as though by prior arrangement, had laid out for private inspection great piles of boiled and smoked sausage, rare confectionery described as 'specialities' (we heard a lot of this little phrase here), 'special fruits', and 'special vegetables'.

Unable to quell the hunger by now welling up within us, which reached its climax at the stand of Turkmenistan's Chardzhous region, we asked the sole representative of Turkmenistan's Agricultural Industry how all these perishable exhibits had been preserved in all their pristine freshness and beauty.

'Easy,' she replied. 'Special teams of workers arrive in Moscow each week with sacks of fruit and vegetables for the exhibition. And I rub the sausages every day with oil.'

At the Ukrainian stand we were told that the exhibition was at present for special guests only, but that regular visitors would be allowed in again as soon as the windows had been glazed.

'Why glazed? So people won't steal the food?' we asked.

'That's right . . .'

Emerging from Pavilion no. 1 and admiring once again the grounded rockets and planes, we tried finally to get a bite to eat. But the cold array of cakes and juices at the food kiosks were in such striking contrast to the epicurean abundance we had just seen that we decided not to bother.

The exhibition in its present form is the embodiment of a vanished era and outmoded thinking. The magnificently sculpted pavilions prove on inspection to be nothing more than rickety wooden barracks with leaking roofs and offices wholly unsuitable for normal work. Simply to maintain these masterpieces of Stalinist architecture in a minimally functional state costs 2.5 million roubles every year. The demonstration of mythical achievements in these pavilions costs the treasury over 20 million roubles a year, and the awarding of medals and other prizes which have long since lost their former prestige accounts for another 12 million. And what do we see in return? A world of ostentation and illusion, whose final result is to debase and degrade us.

It's not just people like us, who have little to do with the exhibition, who think like this. The accelerating tempo of change in our country is forcing a rethink from even the most dedicated of the 6,000 or so workers there.

The first attempt to alter the stereotypes which had developed over the decades was an exhibition of technical teaching methods, which opened in early 1988. In 10,000 square yards of exhibition space visitors were shown not the bright and sunny classrooms of the future, but the reality: the physics sets devised in the memorable year of 1937, with which children still learn the basics of modern physics; the dreary, primitive visual aids; the Soviet teaching computers, whose chief quality appears to be their record number of mistakes per minute. And alongside all this – without comment – are all the long-term official prognostications, which have somehow never been borne out in reality, and the genuine miracles of technical teaching, all affixed with the label 'Made in . . .'. In our view, this exhibit comes closer than anything else to the true state of affairs in our country. More importantly, it inspires a feeling of cathartic shame, which may (and must!) be one of our chief motivating forces for progress. And if shame is to be our motivating force for progress, then so be it.

It must be said that this exhibition made a shocking impression on most visitors, rooted as most of us still are in the stagnant old stereotypes. 'Why should we be shown this nightmare?' people said. 'Make it pretty for us! Show us something that will please our eyes, bathe us in sleep, and divert us from the problems of everyday life.'

But we've had enough of all this! It's time to wake up!

One last thing. We have always assumed that there could be nothing more *open* than an exhibition. But cruel times have done their work here, too. Along with *closed* shops and *closed* offices there has now appeared in our vocabulary the essentially paradoxical idea of *closed* exhibitions. Closed to whom, pray? To visitors? Then it isn't an exhibition at all, but a 'private view'. In just one day at the Exhibition of Economic Achievements we found just two exhibits successfully functioning (or rather *not* functioning). Why not start the overripe process of renewal by *closing down all closed exhibits?*

Must We Rehabilitate Marx?
Semyon Gurevich

Hundreds of books previously hidden away in the special archives of the libraries are soon to be released on to the open shelves, and we shall shortly start republishing the works of Bukharin. Perhaps we can now set up a special commission to rehabilitate Marx . . .

Not long ago two students of mine came up to me at the end of a lecture, and said: 'You've been talking about Marx. Why isn't the Russian translation of his works called the *Complete Works*? Aren't they complete?'

I explained that the translated works of Marx and Engels, although not absolutely complete, gave one a perfectly adequate idea of their writings. The boys nodded in silence, and when I had finished, one of them said quietly: 'We know all that. But why do people say that some of Marx's works haven't been translated into Russian? What about his *Secret Diplomatic History of the Eighteenth Century*? Why aren't we allowed to read it?'

I replied in some embarrassment that I didn't know, but that it must be a mistake which would surely soon be corrected.

At the time I honestly didn't know why only specialists knew about this work, and why one of Marx's major writings, on the history of Russia, had remained unknown to his Russian readers for over a hundred years.

This isn't merely a small article, but a work of several hundred pages, which Marx published between 1856 and 1857 as a series of articles in English newspapers, and which was republished in full after his death by his daughter Eleanor.

The text contains numerous previously unpublished diplomatic documents and pamphlets of the time, which Marx uses as the basis for a survey of Russian history, from the founding of Kievan Rus to the end of the eighteenth century. Despite the occasionally sketchy nature of this survey, its conclusions are important even now in helping us to understand the nature of the historical process which formed the Russian state. Such as his magnificent description of Peter the Great, and his role as a great reformer trying to civilise Russia, and struggling against Asiatic backwardness.

Many of his historical observations we might now disagree with, but his first excursion into historical research laid the basis for his later work on the nineteenth century, and the history and outcome of the revolutionary movement.

Of course, there are many people in the Soviet Union who have read this work in English, and several researchers at the Institute of Marxism-Leninism, aware of the stupidity of the situation, have repeatedly tried to get it published. But they have knocked on many doors and risen higher and higher up the bureaucratic ladder, only to hear the same implacable 'No!' They redoubled their efforts, wrote memoranda, explained and pleaded, all to no avail. Once they were very nearly successful, and a translation was commissioned for inclusion in one of the supplementary volumes of Marx and Engels's works. But at the last moment the same resounding 'No!' intervened from on high.

What were the grounds for these refusals? Those who decided the fate of Marx's work must surely have had some very weighty reasons for consistently refusing to publish it.

It's only recently, since talking to Marxist scholars and remembering how long it took us to republish some of Lenin's later works, that I started to draw a few conclusions for myself.

Marx was not afraid to express his views, and alongside his high opinion of Peter the Great there are also some mercilessly scathing descriptions of the first Russian Tsars. I can well imagine some haughty official's reaction to Marx's claim that the Moscow Tsars 'tatarised' Moscow. Or his sarcastic description of Ivan I's repulsive role as the instrument of the usurping Tatar Khan.

These high officials are guided by feelings of patriotism – a false patriotism, more akin to nationalism than socialist internationalism – according to which the slightest criticism of our country's inadequacies amounts to an attack on the foundations of socialism itself.

How long will this go on? What is to stop the book being issued now, to give all of us the chance to judge it for ourselves?

In the meantime I shall merely have to advise my students, if they know English, to go to the library and read the fifteenth volume of the English edition of Marx and Engels's works.

Cotton Slave
Alexander Treplyov

*Every morning radio stations throughout the Soviet Union
tell us that children are no longer working in the cotton fields
of Central Asia. Living in Moscow, one might be tempted to
believe them. But in fact, little has changed in these primitive
rural economies.*

Four hours by plane and another half an hour by car brought me and
two Uzbek writers to the Srednechirkiks region, near the Uzbek
capital of Tashkent. It was half past two on 14 September 1988, and
the temperature was 40 degrees.

We were too early for the main harvest, we were told. But I knew
that children had been working here this April, and that we would
see them in the fields now. Sure enough, it wasn't long before dozens
of children came pouring through an archway, each of them wearing
a cotton-picking apron.

Last year, they worked every day for two and a half months, they
told me, from nine in the morning until six at night. None of them
knew how long it would last this year. When the cottom was picked
their work would be done and they could go back to school again.

I asked one of them, a boy named Damir, what they had had to eat
that day.

'Breakfast was bread, butter, and tea, sir. Supper was pea soup
and porridge.'

'What about lunch?'

'We didn't get any lunch.'

'And what about yesterday's lunch?'

'Macaroni.'

'With a chop, sir,' added another child. A chop didn't sound so
bad, until I remembered it was autumn in Tashkent, and I wondered
where all the fruit and vegetables were.

Shortly after this we visited another region not far from Tashkent, and went into a school housed in a sweltering dilapidated shack built in the 1930s. Some infants in the playground were drinking water out of a tap. I visited the pleasant director, sitting in his office under a portrait of Lenin. A poster on the wall displaying the names of all the Politburo members had three faces covered up with bits of paper, and when I moved them I saw the names of Kunaev, Yeltsin, and Sokolov.

Going into the class of ten-year-olds I wrote $7 \times 8 = ?$ on the blackboard. A boy came up to the board and wrote 48. I put the same question to a class of seventeen-year-olds, and a girl came up with the answer 54.

Throughout Uzbekistan the highways, streets, and buildings are plastered with enormous posters showing a smiling man bearing handfuls of cotton. The adults smile while the children work. They should either take the posters off the streets or take the children off the fields and back to school.

Cotton slave

Toys for boys

Autumn wedding

The Ultimate Step
I. Vedeneeva

'Nobody could endure what I've been through these last three years. I can't take any more. I'm taking my life . . .'

'Thanks for the "help", Mum. It made me a laughing-stock at school. I'll never forgive you and Dad for putting me through that . . .'

'I'm forty-four. I can't go on with this pointless, humiliating existence . . .'

'Tell Victor he's got what he wanted. He's free now. Let him get on with his life and enjoy himself . . .'

'Yury darling, I've no more strength. My illness has made us all suffer so much. I can't stand any more. I'm very tired. Please don't be sad. This is the best way. Kiss my little Nadya for me, and say Granny's staying with friends . . .'

These are all suicide notes. Thousands of such notes are written every year. Thousands more don't write anything. What impels someone to take their own life? The burdens and humiliations of life, or a surfeit of joy? Friends who betray, or wasted talents? Unattainable desires, or the lack of desires?

We are at Moscow's Sklifosovsky Institute, the only hospital in the capital to treat attempted suicides. People arrive here poisoned or cut down from the noose, but still alive. The ones who die go elsewhere.

They're taken straight to the resuscitation rooms. Pressure chambers, stomach pumps, blood transfusions, sutures. Hundreds of people, men and women, married and divorced, the old and the young, the sick, the healthy, and the homeless – all are equal as they lie lifeless under the white sheet of the operating table. It's not the doctors' job to go into the details of their personal dramas. The doctors' job is to resuscitate them. And they're especially busy in the evening, when the suicide rate shoots up.

Dr Ivan Diky, the institute's director, is up to his eyes in work. Some patients are waiting to be discharged, others need to be examined, the telephone never stops ringing, the ward-round is about to start, and now he has to talk to a journalist . . . Diky answers my questions briskly and without emotion. He has worked here for a long time and he has got used to people who don't want to live. His responsibility is to get them on their feet as quickly as he can. A sheet of paper on the wall above him shows the number of people admitted to the hospital, and the percentage of those who don't survive. It's up to him to make sure this percentage remains as low as possible.

He hands me a white coat, shouts out some instructions to someone, and dashes off to the wards, with me tagging along behind. He takes me to various beds, and I listen in some embarrassment as he tells me matter-of-factly that this one is Vasya. He was no good at work, his wife left, he decided to hang himself – look, there's the scar on his neck. These people wouldn't have had a chance in the past, he says, but these days we can save them with pressure chambers . . . Now here is Olya. Her husband was an alcoholic and beat her, and she had nowhere to go, so she took an overdose . . . And this one is Nikolai, he was bullied by his workmates . . .

Olya, Vasya, Nikolai, and the rest lie there with their bandaged throats, faces, and hands, eyes closed, faces turned to the wall, paying us absolutely no attention, indifferent to whatever the doctor cares to say about them. These are the observation wards, and they are the most difficult ones of all. Here are the patients who have just been brought out of the resuscitation room and need to be closely monitored.

As we move on to new wards and new patients, the doctor continues his running commentary. This poor chap from the back of beyond came to the capital thinking things would be easier here. Little did he know! Couldn't get a job, no one wanted him, couldn't get registered, driven from pillar to post, nothing worked out, so in desperation he decided to throw himself under a train. But even that didn't work out. The train just cut his legs off and left him alive to face a new problem – how to get invalidity benefit without a residence permit. So now he's staying here while the doctors sort things out for him.

Dr Diky waves his arm, and on we go.

'You wouldn't believe how many desperate, messed-up people we've got here,' he says. 'We have to give a lot of them their bus fare when they go, otherwise they'd be stranded here. The problem for most of these people, though, is that they don't have anywhere to go. Meet Nikolai here. He used to sleep in railway stations. When they moved him on he lived rough on the streets. He slept out in the snow and got such a bad case of pneumonia the doctors were amazed it hadn't killed him. How did you manage it, eh, old boy?'

The 'old boy' has evidently long since lost the habit of being addressed as a human being, let alone being taken care of. Terribly thin, with sunken cheeks, a yellow face, and a gaping wound in his chest, he gazes devotedly into the doctor's eyes, nodding his head at him after he leaves . . .

'We also get a fair number of students, many of them from the top universities,' says the doctor, continuing on his round. 'Humanities, arts, technical sciences, the lot. Problem is they're spoilt! Take Marina, that nice-looking young girl over there. She'd almost graduated and her handsome boyfriend had just arrived. What more could you want? But no, she had to put a rope round her neck. She was terrified of living, you see. Afraid to live, but not afraid to hang herself . . .'

The girl with the brushed-back hair and a deep, blue weal on her neck stares silently ahead of her . . .

'There's a professor who recently discharged himself from here. Another doctor, a colleague. It was depression, you see, he just couldn't go on. And take that granny over there. Why would an old lady like her want to die? OK, the young ones don't know anything about life, but her . . . There are a lot of soldiers here too. Can't take their military service. Lot of teenagers, too. Take Olechka here, intelligent girl, doing well at school, played the violin, then invented some high-flier for herself instead of making do with a real-life boy . . .'

We go on. The nurses talk on the telephone. Their resuscitated patients sleep, lie quietly, read, look out of the window, and play chess. Meanwhile new patients keep arriving, with closed eyes and darkened faces. Life goes on as usual in the hospital for those who want to die . . .

Tens of thousands of people kill themselves every year in our country. The figures are appalling, equivalent to the disappearance of whole towns.

For a long time all our suicide statistics were suppressed. In the developed countries in the West and some socialist ones, the figures are regularly published and carefully analysed, to permit the best possible programme to help those who have fallen on hard times. The last time official suicide data were published here, however, was in the 1920s, by the Department of Moral Statistics. This department was closed down in the thirties, and it was only literally a few weeks ago that the information was made available again. Now at last we can see the true picture of events.

Lydia Postovalova, a candidate of philosophy who works at the All-Union Scientific-Methodological Suicidology Centre, helped to explain these figures to me with some data provided by the Ministry of Statistics.

In 1965, 39,550 people killed themselves. The worst year was 1984, when the figure rose to 81,417. The number then declined: in 1985 it was 68,073; in 1986, 52,830; and in 1987, 45,105.

Suicide figures for 1987, by sex and age:

Women		*Men*	
Under 20	522	Under 20	1,672
20–30	1,260	20–30	6,791
30–50	3,436	30–50	16,594
50–70	5,050	50–70	11,725
70+	3,648	70+	3,399
Total	13,916	Total	40,181

'The 1984 peak was followed by a marked decline,' says Postovalova, 'which we attribute to the recent anti-alcohol campaign, since so many suicides are committed under the influence of drink. On the other hand, the suicide rate amongst adolescents and the old has risen dramatically.

'Statistics fail to convey the full picture. Let's say there are 1,275 suicides in Moscow in 1987, 660 in Leningrad, and 210 in Izhevsk. Now it may appear that things are very much better in Izhevsk, but in fact the situation is far more alarming there than in Leningrad, where the rate is 15 per 100,000 of the population, whereas in Izhevsk it's as many as 33 in every 100,000.

'Because the statistics have been concealed for so long and scientists haven't had access to them, there's a lot that's hard to explain, and we have no available data on people's social status, family situation, ethnic origins, state of health, or possible motivations for killing themselves. Take the 1986 statistics for the Latvian Republic, for instance, where more than seventeen times more twenty- to twenty-four-year-old men commit suicide than women. Women of the same age in Tadjikistan in the same year, however, are 1.6 times more likely than men to commit suicide. Why is this? Or consider Udmurtia, which leads the autonomous republics with 41.1 suicides for every 100,000 of the population, almost the same rate as in Hungary, which has the highest suicide rate in the world. But why Udmurtia? Why not neighbouring Mordovia, where the figures for 1986 were just 16.9?

'Then the suicide rate in the countryside has now started to exceed that in the towns. Why is this? Which social groups are most likely to commit suicide in the cities? Only when we have the full picture and can study it as thoroughly as do our Western counterparts can we begin to give effective help to those who need it.'

Lydia Postovalova's Suicidology Centre is attempting to find answers to these and other questions. I asked the Centre's director, Honoured Scientist of the USSR Aina Ambrumova, to tell me about its work.

'We're the centre of a complex of social and psychological welfare offices, a telephone help-line, and the Soviet Union's first crisis clinic. This clinic is very different from the usual psychiatric hospital. We try here to identify people with suicidal tendencies, and to work with those who have already attempted suicide. We have already had some success. Repeated suicide attempts have sharply declined in Moscow thanks to us, and all the evidence points to the high probability of these second attempts, especially in the first year.

'But we still have a lot of problems. The telephone help-line, for instance. For a long time it was referred to very grudgingly as a bourgeois invention, of no possible use to any Soviet citizen, so it's hardly surprising if not as many people know about it as we would like. It operates twenty-four hours a day, seven days a week, and we very much hope that Moscow's example will be followed by other towns, especially places like Sverdlovsk and Arkhangelsk, where the situation is especially worrying.

'But the clinic is our proudest achievement. People in psychological distress come here voluntarily and talk to experienced psychiatrists, and they leave feeling quite different about things . . .'

The clinic is indeed very cosy, with comfortable furniture, discreet lighting, nice curtains, and none of the doctors wearing white coats. It has only thirty beds, and when you consider all the thousands of people trying to kill themselves, thirty beds does seem an awfully small number, even with nice curtains and comfortable furniture. But thank goodness even for them.

It is seven o'clock. Psychiatrists Poleev and Starshenbaum have spent the day teaching their patients to live, and now their working day is over and we sit talking over glasses of tea.

'You think people commit suicide because they don't want to live?' Alexander Poleev asks me. 'Nothing of the sort! Many of them want to live more than you or I. But they can't.

'Take a man we had here recently. He was healthy, good-looking, and enormously strong-willed. Everything had seemed to be going his way. Happily married, two lovely children, interesting job. Then all of a sudden he falls head-over-heels in love with another woman. Forgive me, he says to his wife, I'm off. He gives her everything – flat, furniture, the lot – and moves in with this new woman, with whom he lives happily for a year. Then suddenly she says: "I love you, but I need more out of life," and tells him she's leaving him to marry a diplomat and settle abroad. When our patient walks back that evening to the flat they've shared for a year and sees her and a man silhouetted against the window, he takes several packets of strong sleeping powder and gulps them down with snow. It's only thanks to his strong constitution that he survived at all.

'People kill themselves when they return from the local soviet office, or the shops, or the endless queues, because of the utter frustration and humiliation of it all. This is the grey, mindless, unendurable routine of our everyday lives, from which the more sensitive and emotional of us can see no escape . . .

'For many years doctors in the Soviet Union considered everyone who committed suicide to be mentally ill. The normal, healthy person wants to live, our doctors informed us, and the rest of us went along with them. But the suicide rate is now reaching such epic proportions that if we continue to regard such people as sick we must regard our entire society as sick.

'Things are especially hard nowadays for children and teenagers, and the suicide rate in this age group has recently increased much faster than among adults. Generally neither parents nor teachers can explain why a child killed itself. Everything seemed fine, they say, she was healthy, well-adjusted, well-fed and clothed . . .

'Take Olya K. At three in the afternoon she came home from school as usual, ate the meal that had been left for her, washed her plate, did her maths homework, tidied her folder, opened the window . . . and jumped from the fourteenth floor. A good, quiet little girl, said her parents. Obedient and well-brought-up, said her teachers. A happy child, they all said. But happy children don't throw themselves out of windows! Only later did we learn about her parents' violent rows, the endless shouting at home, her teacher's roughness . . .

'Teenagers, like the old, are suffering increasingly from loneliness,' says Valery Khaikin, the Centre's specialist in adolescent problems. 'Family misunderstandings are exacerbated by housing problems. Most teenagers don't have a room of their own or any chance of privacy, and even if they do, their parents tend to spy on them, demanding to know who they're going around with and so on. Things are often no better at school. With such huge classes, a teacher rarely gets the chance to establish a proper personal relationship with every teenager in her class . . .'

I recalled a Baltic documentary film I saw at a recent festival, about an eleven-year-old boy who took his own life. He lived in a remote little town somewhere, and at first there didn't seem to be anything particularly wrong. He and his little sister had no father. Their mother slaved away all day at a farm, and when she returned home exhausted she would shout at them and sometimes even hit them, as do many mothers in these benighted little towns.

The film-makers didn't seek to prove anything. They didn't blame the mother, half-dead with grief, or go looking for culprits in the school. They simply tried to see through the little boy's eyes the sort of life he had led.

We see the squalid little town, the slush and the washed-away roads. We see his mother getting up at dawn and setting off for the farm. We see the bus, the sleepy, exhausted passengers in their boots, and the dirty farm. We see the phone ringing in the flat as the mother wakes up her daughter. We see the food on the stove, the radio blaring out its usual monotonous news, the walk to school and the walk back home again. We see the mother, cold and tired, an unappetising meal on the table, hands rough with work, ugly clothes, the occasional unloving boyfriend, the mother weeping, shouting, exhausted . . . Homework, the dreary landscape outside the window, then television and sleep. And tomorrow will be exactly the same, and so will the day after, and the day after that . . .

It could have been the mother herself, but she's resigned to her life. The little boy refused to resign himself to it and killed himself.

'To take one's life under the influence of some unbearable inner crisis is something of which only the very rare, exceptionally noble soul is capable,' Einstein wrote.

Yet suicide is also something none of us has the right to judge. To try to help and understand is another matter. We are only just beginning to realise how little we understand human psychology.

Our country, despite the promise of its slogan 'All in the name of the People!', appears in fact to have done very little for its people. No amount of achievements in science and technology, agriculture and industry, the ballet and space travel, can help someone to understand themselves and others. None of these things can help us to live, and to find solutions to the emotional crises which beset us.

We must look after our people. Otherwise a new night will fall, and hundreds will decide that they no longer want to live . . .

Afghanistan: The Balance-Sheet
Artyom Borovik

Ogonyok *has provided a platform for widely varying views on the war in Afghanistan. Our correspondent recently talked in Kabul to General Valentin Ivanovich Varennikov, a leading advocate of a political solution in Afghanistan, who has headed the Ministry of Defence Operations Group there for the past four years, and who virtually masterminded the withdrawal of Soviet troops between 1986 and 1989.*

General Varennikov's military record is an impressive one. Born in 1923 in Krasnodar, he joined the Soviet Army in 1941, and left for the front in October 1942 in command of a platoon. He was later appointed deputy commander of an artillery regiment, and fought in Poland, the Ukraine, Stalingrad, and Berlin. In 1971 he became deputy Commander-in-Chief of Soviet forces in the GDR. Eight years later he was appointed to the General Staff, and in 1989 he was made Deputy Minister of Defence and Commander-in-Chief of Soviet land forces.

We now know that the General Staff was opposed to sending troops into Afghanistan from the start, but that the Ministry of Defence, headed by Dmitry Ustinov, overrode them. How was it that those without any special military training were able to ignore the advice of their General Staff?

'It's true that Marshal Ogarkov, then head of the General Staff, and his deputy, Marshal Akhromeev, were both fiercely opposed to the invasion. But I don't think we can blame Ustinov alone for this. He was simply in the wrong place at the wrong time. Nor must we judge the decision in the context of the totally different political scene today. Gorbachev's global peace initiatives have fundamentally altered the course of international relations, particularly Soviet–US relations. Ten years ago the world situation was quite different, and superpower relations were dominated by suspicion and mistrust. This confrontation became especially dangerous towards the end of the 1970s, and had an enormous influence on political decision-making in Washington and Moscow.

'Despite all this, our main purpose in sending troops into Afghanistan was merely to stabilise the situation there. This was why the General Staff wanted Soviet units to go in as garrison forces, to help the local population with supplies and so forth, and to support them against guerrilla attacks. We were also adamant that our forces should not be increased.

'For a whole series of reasons our troops became more and more embroiled in military activity, and it was finally decided to increase our military presence, but it's now clear that the General Staff's line was essentially correct, even though it created serious problems for us at the time. If our army had gone in as garrison units in the first place, we could have made contact with the local population in the towns and villages, and a great many losses on both sides could have been avoided. We did achieve this in a number of regions, despite the war, and our units managed to put down roots in a number of places, often averting conflicts between government and opposition troops. I myself made many visits to these regions, where I met opposition commanders and their men. There was nothing to stop them shooting a Soviet general, yet they never did, and this in itself lent weight to our garrison theory. We should have made these peaceful contacts our ammunition, instead of getting mixed up with Babrak Karmal and letting ourselves get dragged into a long-drawn-out war.

'Whenever we met Karmal, he would always listen most attentively to everything we had to say, and take notes, and at the end of our discussion he would say: "You must be thinking 'This Karmal writes and writes, but he does nothing . . .'" This was unfortunately all too true. Karmal never won the trust of either his colleagues, his people, or his Soviet advisers. He was a supreme demagogue and faction-fighter, who excelled at dressing himself up in revolutionary phrases. It was these talents that gave him his charisma. After each new catastrophe he would assure everyone: "*Now* I see where I went wrong, comrades! There will be no more mistakes!" And each time we believed him, and waited for things to change. Meanwhile he split the party from top to bottom, never bothered to get people to work with him, and turned both party and government into the bureaucratic machine which is there to this day.

'Unfortunately many people were hoodwinked by Karmal, even though by 1982 he was clearly making some major political blunders. One need only look at his economic and social policies, notably his disastrous land and water reforms and his approach to religion. At the time he simply paid lip-service to traditional tribal customs and the power of Islam, and issued endless slogans calling for radical socialist transformation, even though the conditions for this simply did not exist. None of it was done in bad faith, of course, but simply out of incompetence and inertia.

'By jumping the gun in this way, the Kabul government alienated people from the revolution, and instead of integrating Islam into their policies they allowed religion to fall into the hands of the opposition, which made good use of it. So it's not surprising that so many mullahs ended up in the opposition camp, and that religious leaders became rebel leaders. This was particularly so in areas like Kandahar, led by mullahs Nakib, Nasim, Malang, Fatsanei, and co.

'Karmal continued systematically cutting the tree from under him and compromising the Afghan People's Democratic Party. Meanwhile many of our Soviet advisers, who were working to support the leaders of the APDP and avert possible calamity, failed to assess the situation properly. Many of them were woefully ignorant of Asian affairs, and their activities all too often reflected the dogmatism of the stagnation era.

'There are many reasons why we trusted Karmal. But the main one is that the APDP had no choice, and our people in Kabul then fully supported them. Another reason is that throughout the seventies and early eighties our officials tended to report back only the information which they thought would please Moscow.

'This reporting of "pleasant" information is unfortunately a common symptom of the disease of stagnation, and is not limited to diplomacy. It meant that Moscow often made the wrong decisions. For instance, they rejected the idea of several autonomous regions within a united Afghanistan, because they were afraid the country would collapse, even though such a scheme would have significantly reduced tension between central government and local leaders. It's also obvious now that we should have agreed much earlier to an open dialogue with the opposition leaders, both within Afghanistan and abroad.

Afghan veteran at a Kiev military hospital

'The old dogmatism, inertia, and clumsiness did our country untold harm. Things are very different now. We can go about our work more calmly, and we can now be sure that the newspapers we read will contain the truth rather than half-truths.

'The present Afghan government under Najibullah is doing its best to clear up the mess, even though wreckers and saboteurs are still active in both government and opposition. It's desperately important for the party to maintain solidarity as we withdraw our troops; the opposition would pounce on the slightest show of disunity.

'Afghanistan's armed forces now consist of around 300,000 trained soldiers, and a command structure experienced in organising and conducting military manoeuvres. We've given them a vast amount of ammunition, supplies, and modern military technology – tanks, armoured personnel-carriers, artillery, military and transport planes, and so forth. The opposition has nothing like this, of course, and never will have . . .'

One problem seems to be that Soviet advisers have often simply replaced Afghans in their jobs. Last summer I met the editor of a major Kabul newspaper, who had only the haziest notion of the mechanics of publishing because our advisers did it all for him. Was there a similar problem in the army? I wondered.

'After April 1978, Afghans from all walks of life entered the party, the government, and the army. Some proved totally unsuited to their new jobs; they knew next to nothing, worked carelessly, lacked the most elementary understanding of the APDP's programme, and were clearly only in it for the money. This was why some of our advisers often found it easier to do things themselves rather than get their Afghan counterparts to do them.

'The other reason for this passivity, of course, is that the country is being torn apart by a civil war in which brothers may stand on opposite sides of the barricades. Family intrigues, which frequently still exist in the most bizarre forms, have inevitably left their mark on those in the party, the government, and the army.

'It was as more and more regions were being engulfed in this civil war that we tried to abandon military solutions in favour of a political one. This change has naturally to be seen in the context of everything else that was going on in the Soviet Union then, starting with the

April 1985 plenum of the Party Central Committee, when Mikhail Gorbachev was elected General Secretary. Taking stock of the hopeless situation in Afghanistan, Gorbachev announced a new political approach to the problem, and declared that the priority from now on would be to save lives and reduce casualties. All this happened shortly after I arrived permanently in Afghanistan, and we started immediately to review the whole basis of our operations there.

'All through 1985, and especially in 1986, we received constant communiqués on these lines from Moscow. I remember our endless discussions in Kabul about the need to tackle problems politically, and our detailed analyses of various solutions to different problems. There were enough Afghans and Soviets who supported a political solution at that time. Military intervention is a primitive way of settling this kind of question. But the alternatives require huge patience, determination, and skill, and sadly we lacked the strength to defend this line. Stark necessity forced us to continue military action, and most of our discussions at the time got nowhere.

'There were frequent changes at the top in our Kabul offices, but it seemed to me as though every new person would start afresh from exactly the same position: "Soviets and Afghans must organise huge joint military operations against the guerrillas. Only then will the Afghan people be able to live in peace!"

'The point is that the vast majority of the Afghan people aren't guerrillas at all, just local men arming themselves to defend their tribal interests. I could name numerous regions where people don't support the government but won't allow opposition troops on to their territory either. They have always treasured their independence, and naturally attack anyone who arrives to impose authority on them. In backing the Afghan leadership in the early years of the war, we assumed that we would have to "implant" its organisational nucleus into the various provinces. But people wouldn't allow this "popular" power into their villages, so military units would be sent in to defend it and our Afghan comrades would rush in to tell us that one district after another had been "liberated from bandits". This was clearly absurd, but these are hot-headed Oriental people, and it took a lot of time to convince them that this sort of thing merely harmed us and helped the enemies of the revolution.

'With the start of the new policy in 1987, Commissions for Reconciliation were set up throughout the country. Our military tactics didn't change overnight, and we still had to restrain our Afghan comrades from embarking on more military actions. But Soviet troops gradually managed to improve relations with the people in quite a number of regions, and in the end they were able to mix quite freely not just with the local people, but with those whom our press had previously described as "bandits".

'We did all we could to help the leadership reconcile local government and opposition forces, and in a number of regions, such as Herat, we were successful. Not only there, either. The west and south-west of the country now tend to be quite peaceful, even though things there had previously been extremely tense.

'One could illustrate the need for this sort of political approach by looking at the defence of the frontier. The border between Pakistan and Afghanistan, the so-called "Durand Line", passes through an area populated by resettled Pathans. The people living on either side of this line are bound together by history, traditions, and tribal relationshps, so it's important that they guard their own bit of this notional frontier themselves, and this is how things were under the King.

'The fact that reconciliation has been much harder in the east is partly due to the inflexibility of the Peshawar government. But there were other reasons, too. In the west, for instance, we established excellent working relationships with many of the local governors. The governor of Herat, a certain Khaikyar, is a wise, highly educated, far-sighted man, and a member of the local tribe. Although not a party member, he managed to win over quite a number of armed detachments to the government side, and the local opposition leader, Turan Ismail, never succeeded in luring them back. Then there's the governor of Helmend province, a man named Shakhnazar, who has become a personal friend. He was the leader of an armed opposition group, but went over to the government side. He isn't without his faults, of course, but he has always pursued the correct line to stop the fighting in his province. So many people in Afghanistan today are driven by personal grudges and ambitions, rather than the desire to work with both sides for peace.

'When our Afghan comrades announced their national reconciliation policy, they envisaged a broad-based coalition government which would end the war. Of course we support this idea totally – there's no alternative. There are naturally some who refuse to work with this government unless the APDP is excluded. But this is just foolish. Like it or not, the APDP has guided the government for the past ten years; it controls all the organs of state, including the armed forces, and it guarantees its foreign policies.

'Many people say now that we didn't defend our position strongly enough during the Geneva peace negotiations, and that the resulting agreements were lopsided. Those negotiations lasted for several years, and have come to nothing. Our main problem was somehow to swing the opponents of peace and talk them into signing the agreements. Our negotiators were understandably afraid that if their conditions were too harsh they might drive these people into a corner.

'We tried to get all parties to accept the principle of "parity". Shortly before our troops left, there were 183 Soviet military installations on Afghan territory, and 181 opposition bases, headquarters, training schools, and so on in Pakistan. Since both sides had roughly the same number of installations, the United Nations could have overseen a programme of balanced force reductions. We undertook to withdraw all our troops by 15 February 1989, and this we have done. Pakistan undertook to destroy all opposition bases on its territory, but it has not only not done so, it hasn't even allowed UN troops to inspect them. World opinion is therefore entitled to demand that the USA and Pakistan fulfil their side of the Geneva agreements.'

I asked General Varennikov when the heaviest fighting had been, and which military operations had made the greatest impression on him.

'The heaviest fighting was in late 1984 and early 1985, just as we were moving towards a political solution in Afghanistan. The most impressive military manoeuvre must be the Kunar operation of 1985, in which battles raged along the entire eighty miles of the fiercely defended Kunar gorge, from Jalalabad to Barikot, taking in the mountain spur of the Pechdat gorge. During the operation over 11,000 Soviet troops were landed in helicopters, but not one of our helicopters was destroyed, even though the guerrillas had just started using American and British Stinger and Blowpipe missiles.

'1986 was memorable for the battles in the province of Paktiya and for the Parachinar salient, but mainly for our attack on the insurgents' base at Djavara, in the mountain range of the Khost region, near the Pakistan frontier. This base had taken ten years to construct, was built according to the latest rules of modern fortification, and embodied all the power of the opposition forces in the south-east. Djavara was generally regarded as impregnable, but in the end not even the guerrillas' massive modern Western anti-aircraft devices could save them.

'1986 was also the year of a successful Afghan–Soviet operation to the west of Herat, taking in the arsenal base of Kakari-Shashari, near the Iranian frontier. This wiped out the main opposition forces in that area, and resulted in a huge exodus of guerrilla units to the government side.

'The following year we organised military operations around Kandahar, the most difficult area in the whole of Afghanistan. The rebels here had been having things their own way and terrorising the local population. The local Commission for Reconciliation was destroyed three times, schools were closed, and shops and government offices worked only with the rebels' permission. So between April and September we organised joint operations to wipe out the most tenacious opposition forces in Kandahar and the adjoining districts of Argandab, Pandzhvai, and Daman.

'Conditions were tough, the enemy was strong, the terrain was difficult, and the temperature was never below 50 degrees in the shade. But we smashed them. Our troops cordoned off the whole area, while Afghan units, backed by Soviet fire-power, moved in and cleared them out. Six months have passed, and the local government is still holding its own.

'Then at the end of 1987, the joint Soviet–Afghan Operation Highway opened up and secured the strategic road from Gardez to Khost, making the town accessible to anyone who needed it.'

Soviet troops have been withdrawn from Afghanistan in three separate phases: in the autumn of 1986, in the summer of 1988, and between January and February 1989. Which of these phases was the most difficult?

'The first was before the end of the Geneva negotiations, and the other two were on the basis of the agreement reached there. The autumn 1986 withdrawal was something quite new. The government decided that we would withdraw six regiments, and while they were getting ready to leave, our military intelligence people discovered that opposition extremists at the behest of the Alliance 7 group were planning a bloodbath for us.

'We naturally had to take counter-measures. Two weeks before we were due to leave, we announced the date of our withdrawal and the precise route our units would be taking. We also kept a close watch on opposition troops, who were massing around the lines of communication. Afghan and Soviet forces then bombarded them with artillery and air fire, and we put back the date of our departure. Ten days later we had to repeat the process even more fiercely, since the rebels appeared not to have got the message. That second time they suffered exceptionally heavy losses, as did a large number of foreign military advisers, who I am sure were behind the whole thing.

'A lot was said about this at the time in the Soviet media. We gave the rebels one last warning, and those who wanted a fight were told that if they opened fire we would throw everything we had at them. These harsh measures finally paid off. Our first six regiments got out in 1986 without a scratch. And our troop withdrawals in 1988 and 1989 passed off without any loss of life or equipment.'

General Varennikov daily faces the risk of death in battle or terrorist attack. How does he adjust psychologically to the idea of his own imminent death? Does he ever have time to relax?

'I worked out my own personal tactics during the Second World War. When danger looms and I see an enemy soldier coming for me, I am overwhelmed by a rage that obliterates every other emotion. All of us – ordinary soldiers, NCOs, and officers alike – must be trained to overcome fear and know how to take calculated risks.

'When we first came to Kabul, we agreed to work around the clock, without any days off. Our working day here is officially from 7 a.m. to 10 p.m., but we frequently work through the night.

'Of course, I try to relax by keeping up with the newspapers. People can no more live without the press nowadays than they can without food or air . . .'

When There's No Choice
Andrei Popov

During my student years at one of Moscow's gynaecological hospitals, I met a young woman at the abortion clinic who had come for an operation commonly known as a 'scrape'. For her first 'grown-up' operation, she had come dressed in her Pioneer uniform, of white shirt and red tie.*

I have since learnt that the problem of teenage pregnancies is one of the most urgent health-care problems facing us today.

One in five Soviet women of childbearing age has an abortion every year, and thirty abortions are performed on every hundred women between the ages of fifteen and twenty. Six of these women will have had their first abortion before they are twenty. In Moscow, between 70 and 80 per cent of local women and up to 90 per cent of village women will unofficially terminate their first pregnancies.

My other memories of my student years are of the forensic medicine course, and of the innumerable babies' bodies found during the winter in the Sokolniki and Izmailov parks. Mum would go out for a walk with the baby, and come back alone . . .

For most people here, 'family planning' means constant abortions and the endless search for a coil that fits. It also means abandoned or murdered babies, post-abortion infertility, extramarital pregnancies and the fear of pregnancy.

Parents' right to choose how many children they want, and when, is enshrined in Article 16 of the International Declaration of Human Rights, signed in 1968 in Teheran and the Soviet Union. To make good this right, our government promised to provide us with contraception, information, and medical advice on birth control methods. Twenty years have passed, and the only result of all this

---

* The Pioneer organisation is for children aged between ten and sixteen.

information and contraception is more abortions. And not just abortions, but a deliberate propaganda campaign to bully women about their dangers.

This is quite unnecessary. Women are frightened enough of them as it is, since the preferred Soviet methods of dilation and evacuation, or dilation and curettage, are generally performed without an anaesthetic. But they have no choice. Popular articles and leaflets, not to mention understocked chemist's shops, uninformed local doctors, and insensitive partners, give women few dignified alternatives, or the chance to choose safer contraceptive methods. These alternatives still remain in the realms of lofty scientific abstraction, bearing little relation to the reality of women's lives.

According to WHO statistics, roughly 30 million abortions are performed in the world every year. The Soviet Union accounts for 8 million of these – one in four – even though we make up only 5 to 6 per cent of the world's population. The Soviet abortion rate is two to four times higher than in the European socialist countries, and six to ten times higher than in the West. But specialists here conservatively estimate that abortions performed outside hospitals account for anything between 50 and 100 per cent of those registered. It would be foolish to describe these unofficial abortions as illegal. As a speaker in the GDR remarked during a recent parliamentary debate on the legalisation of abortion: 'A law which makes criminals of almost nine hundred thousand women every year is not a law.'

How is it that the Soviet Union, which led the world in the 1920s in its approach to family planning, is now the only country in the world to use abortion as its main method of birth control? It all started in the 1930s, when the state desperately needed labour and military resources, and the birth rate was falling. The obvious solution was to ban abortions, and in effect contraception too. Thus in 1936 a new law made abortions illegal, and contraceptive research and promotion was virtually curtailed.

Abortions were legalised again in 1956. But the right to contraception, although never strictly speaking banned, was never fully restored.

The contraceptive methods now used by 80 per cent of the population are best described as ineffective, inaccessible, injurious to the health, and virtually indistinguishable from what was available in the thirties. This explains why at least half of all pregnancies in the cities are unplanned, with the result that one Moscow woman in four will prefer the distress of regular abortions to the fear of an unwanted pregnancy and the inconvenience of using traditional contraceptive methods.

So why do we have no modern effective contraception?

Three-quarters of all women who tried to buy contraceptives in 1980 came out of the chemist's shop empty-handed. But these are nationwide averages, and the overall figure of 25 per cent may mean a 75 per cent success rate in Moscow, and only 5 per cent in a town like Krasnoyarsk.

So what do our doctors and health officials have to say?

Every year sees new routine directives from the Ministry of Health on the need to reduce the abortion rate. Meanwhile the Deputy Minister of Health for Children's Affairs, A. G. Gracheva, expressed her concern for the problem of abandoned babies in a recent article for *Soviet Russia*. 'We have petitioned the Ministry of Justice to issue a draft decree from the Presidium of the Supreme Soviet,' she writes, 'which would provide genetic counselling, the compulsory investigation of all couples wishing to marry, and the compulsory termination of pregnancy for all women alcoholics and drug addicts.'

So that's it. I very much hope that forcible sterilisation won't become the law. Or state eugenics. I would like to know if leading officials at the Ministry of Health are aware of the dangerous historical precedents for such legislation.

The only way to reduce the number of abortions and unwanted pregnancies is through the wide distribution of modern effective contraceptive methods, under the democratic control of a Soviet Family Planning Association.

But there's a hitch. Soviet women now pay between 50 and 100 roubles not for their own health, or for the health of society as a whole, but for an operation which provides many obstetricians and gynaecologists with a steady source of extra income.

Of course not all doctors make money on abortions. Most of them hate the situation as much as anyone else. But our gynaecological services are at present geared almost exclusively to performing abortions and battling with the ensuing complications. Almost half of our 60,000 gynaecologists – the largest number in the world – perform nothing but abortions, and the average gynaecologist carries out no less than two to three each day. A third of all gynaecological beds are reserved for abortion cases, and half of all women having the operation will have to return to the hospital later on with complications.

Although one operation costs about 100 roubles, the state subsidises them to the tune of a billion roubles each year, a twentieth of the country's total annual health budget.

Now it is clear why our infant mortality rate is three or four times higher than in any other European country: our gynaecologists simply don't have enough time or money left for other problems.

The time has come for a single specialised self-financing family planning service. This new Soviet Family Planning Association will naturally be responsible for abortions too. But being self-financing, it won't be paid for out of the state budget, and will therefore be the only service within the Ministry of Health which is genuinely committed to preventing abortions.

We have the resources, the people, the money, the organisational structure, and even the draft constitution for the new association. We merely have to redirect our gynaecological services from routine abortions towards their prevention. It's that 'merely', of course, which is the problem.

Under Siege
Dmitry Likahnov

He came into our office, sank exhausted into a chair, and said: 'Right, I'll tell you everything. I've had it.'

He isn't much more than thirty. In the past he had set up his own business selling off things on the side, and the times being what they were, he had to operate underground, rejected by society, permanently afraid, and punished with the full force of the law.

Then he opened a co-operative, and for the first time in his life he had something to live for. But the problems remained. And so did the fear. He'd finished with the underground. Co-operatives were perfectly legal, and the government was right behind them. So what was he afraid of?

'I'm talking about organised crime on a massive scale. You know, criminals nosing around people with money, and creaming it off them. It involves every single middleman, dealer, and prostitute working in the state sector, and it includes co-operatives. We all pay up from the word go.

'Organised crime is as old as the black market itself. But everything is different now. When the Beryozka hard-currency shops were closed down a mass of crooks and petty speculators suddenly appeared, with time on their hands. Thousands of these people had been making good money filching receipts, and if money got tight they would go on to outright robbery. Send them to prison fifteen times and they still wouldn't get a proper job. So the moment co-operatives opened, they made a grab for them – particularly the catering ones.

'We'd only been going five months when a thick-looking bloke came up to one of our saleswomen and said that if she didn't bring him 2,000 roubles the next day, she and her family would regret it. We managed to get a friend in to sort him out and everything has been OK so far, but I don't expect it will last, and anyway what sort of way is this to defend ourselves?

'It's definitely the co-operative shops and eating places which will suffer most. They're exposed and have plenty of ready cash. It's one thing for someone I don't know to approach me in the street. But a thousand people pass through a café in a day, and there's no knowing if one of them is carrying a bomb, or plans to cut you up with a knife. And even if you did get three armed policemen posted at the door, you'd have to be sure they didn't get in on the act too . . .

'From what I've heard, gangsters have got their hands on almost every co-operative café and restaurant in Moscow, as well as a number of shops and clothing co-operatives. Soon they'll be in control of the whole co-operative movement.

'You only have to go to the Riga market and see some of the odd-looking types prowling around. Every single trader there is paying them protection money. And the stuff they sell – cigarettes, condoms, spirits, foreign clothes, even drugs and guns. It's rampant speculation. A packet of cigarettes will cost you twenty roubles. A bottle of whisky forty or fifty, a tin of caviare thirty, condoms twenty-five. And women too. You can buy women anywhere. The prostitutes outside the Nationale and Continentale hotels are more choosy and won't go for Soviet money. But the ones everywhere else are for mass consumption, and at the markets people buy them like sacks of potatoes.

'At one time people could make a decent living at the Riga, and it was known throughout the country. The money's not so bad even now, and people still come from all over the Soviet Union. But many others I know have been forced out.

'Someone might spend 100 roubles of his own money to make ten pairs of trousers, and take them off to the market to sell. Then someone comes up to him and says: "Give us 500 roubles!" If he refuses, they'll beat him up, take it off him, and run off. So he pays up, and the next time more people approach him demanding yet more money. This sort of thing goes on everywhere, but at the Riga market it's got completely out of hand.

'As well as all this, you'll have to pay them for a stall. But there are so many people wanting one that you'll have to start queuing at six in the morning. But there's not really any point in trying to get in, which is why you always see the same faces there.

'The gangsters running the Riga are a force to be reckoned with. I've heard certain names mentioned, such as the boys from Long Ponds, and Lyubertsy. And I'm sure the strongest will eventually get total control of the place.

'Then there's Luzhniki. I don't know whose gang is running that at present. Some of them recently appeared and beat up anyone who refused to pay, and in the end everyone did. Thirty roubles each, multiplied by forty. That's over 1,000 roubles every day!

'Since there are several thousand co-operatives in the country these gangsters must be handling huge sums. For instance, when the Beryozka shops were winding up, special shops were opened for

Afghan veterans. Since televisions and videos were getting more and more expensive at the time, a friend of mine decided to do a little black-market business. The "Afghan Beryozka" had 300 television sets and he was one of the first five in the queue, but he didn't get one because a big gang of thugs came in, threw the invalids out of the shop, and swiped the lot. Animals, my friend said they were.

'These 300 televisions were immediately resold at various Beryozka shops in Asia and Moscow. Three hundred television sets means over 450,000 roubles in one day. Even if there are a lot of these bandits, they'll still have more than enough to go round.'

So roughly how many people are involved?

'Thousands. Especially in Moscow. People come here from all over the country. It's a big town. You can hide out without a permit for years, driving around in stolen cars and getting along fine as long as you don't commit some traffic offence. Besides, you can always try to buy your way out of trouble if you're arrested. So I imagine there must be several thousand people involved in organised crime in the capital. One man told me he could get 800 of them together within an hour simply by phoning around all the sports stadiums in Lyubertsy – they're guaranteed to be packed full of them.

'I've seen one of these gangs on their way to some bust-up. They were terrifying! Great big blokes, with huge bull necks. They'd smash your face in just like that.

'But 90 per cent of these louts don't really understand what they're doing, or what the consequences might be. They just get paid 1,000 roubles, and want to make sure they earn it. The brains behind the whole thing, though, are something else, and they keep well away.'

How does the criminal underworld regard these gangsters?

'The tradition is that a thief shouldn't resort to extortion, and that it humiliates and discredits him, and is incompatible with his code of honour. But nowadays there's nothing they won't do. Maybe there's some criminal elite which keeps away from organised crime and just rakes money off other thieves. It's possible, I don't know. Everything's topsy-turvy these days.

'Recently a man I know came back from a prison camp and said that co-operatives were the only thing on their minds there – and he didn't mean how to get a job in one. So I suppose released convicts will soon be joining forces with these gangsters. But the main change is that racketeering is going to get more and more sophisticated, with less and less need for violence.

'Say I have a friend who wants some fur to make jackets. He won't find anything through official channels, of course, and up comes some individual who makes several rather irregular proposals, such as: "I can give you fur, but the kind you want costs forty, and I can get it for you for twenty." These people are crafty, you see. They'll go all out to get something, knowing all the loopholes in the market and exploiting them to the full. And once they get a taker they can name their price. If they're sensible they'll share it out; if not, they'll try and keep the lot.

'At the end of this year, though, things are going to get really rough. Every co-operative will then be allowed to withdraw their profits from the bank and share it out amongst themselves as rewards and bonuses and so on.

'Mark my words, these gangs are going to force people to withdraw their money whether they want to or not, and hand it over. You won't be able to outwit them by leaving it in the bank, and they're sure to kill someone to make their point.'

Can't these people be taught a lesson, as they were recently at Moscow's Vnukovo airport?

'There are a number of especially good spots for private taxi-drivers, Vnukovo airport being one of them. As a rule the same people get these spots, and they're the ones who get all the best fares. So one day the gangsters turned up in their cars and said: "Pay up!" Everywhere else in the town they were demanding anything between 150 and 300 roubles. But taxi-drivers are a different kettle of fish, and handy with a spanner too. So about a thousand of them gathered at Vnukovo to teach the crooks a lesson. "You know our cars, and we know yours," they said. "You burn one of ours and we'll burn one of yours. You smash one of our skulls and we'll smash one of yours!"

'Terrific, they were. But I expect the gangsters will just find ways to pick them off one by one. A thug will come up to someone and tell him to pay up, and he does. Then another tells the same man to pay him instead. "Sort it out amongst yourselves," the man says. "I can't pay you both." So the two of them battle for power, getting supporters, buying guns, paying bodyguards to protect them, and paying their supporters too.

'Meanwhile you and your family don't know from one day to the next what's going to happen to you. So co-operatives have absolutely no way out. They have to pay. Take ours, for instance. We don't steal. We do everything by the book. And we have no money to pay them. That means we have to steal. From ourselves. We have to buy cotton without entering it into the books, and get it made up on the side.

'If the state won't protect its citizens, the results will be catastrophic. Many co-operative managers will go back to the black market, because the alternatives are so dangerous.

'I'm convinced now that a special military unit must be posted on Petrovka Street, with power to shoot. If some gangster gets a bullet in the head, maybe that'll make the others stop and think. I'm not a cruel man. But violence is the only language these people understand, and it's ridiculous to be soft on them.

'Things are bad now, but they're going to get a lot worse. One of our main problems is that although the law on co-operatives says we're doing respected and prestigious work, most people actually think "The bastards are holding Moscow to ransom!" So the last thing anyone wants to do is stick their neck out for us.

'Most people regard us managers as thieves and gangsters. Co-operatives won't last, they say, the government must have let them through on the nod. What these people don't understand, though, is that we can't live without co-operatives, they're our only chance . . .

'Countless government officials are not only opposed to co-operatives but are involved in a vast official racket. The first thing an official thinks about when he meets someone from a co-operative is what he stands to gain, and he conceals his own financial interests by inventing all sorts of interests of state. The result is that we can't buy or sell a thing without bribing someone. You go into a shop which you know has quantities of some material you want to buy. You ask for 500 metres, and they say they can't let you have any, you'll have to talk to the manager. And when you go in to see him, he refuses point-blank to sell it, and that's that. He hasn't enough, there are others who need it, there's not enough to go round, and so on. Yet the minute you slip him some money he'll let you have whatever you want.

'I once tried to buy 200 metres of material. I went to the manager, and he gave me the telephone number of a certain market, where I was told that co-operatives weren't allowed any more than 20 metres. They also said there were some special shops set aside for co-operatives, and they gave me the address. I didn't have much time, but I went along to one of these shops, where they told me they hadn't got anything. Yet I could see with my own eyes that the stuff had just arrived from the factory and was piled up to the ceiling. I refused on principle to give them any money, so I wasted the whole day and went home empty-handed.

'I eventually got what I wanted by greasing a few palms at another shop. What else could I do? If you refuse, people won't talk to you, won't sign your documents, won't give you a single machine or scrap of thread. I was in a factory once when some gang leaders stormed in and smashed some of its machines before my eyes, just because they couldn't agree on a price. Those machines would have suited our co-operative fine: we could have repaired them and they would have lasted us a hundred years. But they were a write-off.

'And the reason we have to buy equipment, rather than hire it, is that the hire-firms demand money on top of the rental money to make the equipment work for them and bring them in a profit. It's usury!

'It's happening everywhere. Take thread. There's none to be had, and no one wants to sell it wholesale. At one time I used to be able to buy as much as we needed. But now I have to grease endless palms. In the old days we had to pay just the director. Now it's his deputy, and the chief engineer, and the head of the planning department, and the head book-keeper. Someone who's never taken a bribe in his life only has to hear the word "co-operative" and he'll come running up for his share. So how am I supposed to get hold of the 200, 300, 500, or 1,000 roubles I need to pay them? Easy. Take it out of the bank, or steal it.

'This is why co-operatives' expenses far exceed their income. It's terrifying how deep-seated it's become! No one is shocked by it any more. When I slip someone some money I try to make sure no one's around to see. But a lot of people just take the money out of their pocket and count it without even looking round, and hand it over in full view of everyone. In the early days of the co-operative movement we used to dream about business with honour. Now all that's gone.

'The law on co-operatives is a complete muddle too, and doesn't say what's allowed and what isn't, so you can interpret any article of it exactly as you see fit. I went to the bank yesterday to arrange an urgent loan. The bank made me three separate offers. Either I could have the money on condition that they took 15 per cent of the profits. Alternatively I could pay them back 150 roubles a month. And the third option was to repay 5 to 10 per cent of the loan. And that's after the principal itself has been cleared, along with the percentage we have to pay the government anyway for some sort of mythical "consultation", which I don't need but have to pay for if I'm to get a loan.

'And then there's all the toing and froing with the district authorities. It's quite easy to register a co-operative nowadays. But after that you have to tackle the district executive committee thirty-eight times a day. You have to get permission from the health department, the fire authorities, and the architect, who all say you can't do this and you can't do that.

'But of course you always can . . .

'If ever I do come across someone who just signs the bit of paper without asking for anything in return, it throws me into a state of shock all day, and I wonder what on earth the catch is.

'The police aren't involved in it yet, thank God. And that's because they haven't been authorised to investigate it thoroughly. But as soon as they are, I'm afraid we shall just have one more group of people to pay.'

So what can we do?

'Before we even started to set up co-operatives we should have organised our wholesale market properly, and thought through the whole question of supplies and sales.

'Now I reckon the government will have to launch a top-level investigation. I can tell you honestly that if I'd known earlier what the consequences would be, I'd have lived a quiet life and kept clear of the whole thing.

'I don't want to be afraid for my family, my child, myself, and my work. Someone offered me a gun some time ago. I didn't have the stomach for it then, but if I get the opportunity again I shall definitely buy myself a pistol . . .'

Patrolling the
Drug Smugglers' Path
Konstantin Smirnov

The path between the frontiers is steep, but the temptations are great when the value of a human life is weighed against a load of opium.

We arrived just before dusk. We had left the border patrol station in the morning, and by six that evening we had covered the fifty miles to the frontier post.

Here in the foothills of the Hindu Kush spring had only just arrived, but the land was already flooded with rain; by the end of May this brief burst of green would be over, the grass would have withered, and scorching winds would be raising clouds of dust and rustling the dry stalks of the thistles.

Our jeep bravely negotiated the mountain track, swerving up perilous vertical slopes, plunging into deep inclines on its side, skidding through twisting ruts, and finally bringing us to a rocky plateau from which we could see the distant outlines of the frontier post.

As we drove on, a young soldier ran up to the car and saluted the officer accompanying us. 'Who's in charge?' asked our guide tersely, opening the car door.

'The Political Education Officer.'

'Where's the boss and Captain Konev?'

'Left on the night patrol,' replied the soldier, peering up at the darkening sky.

The officer slammed the door shut, and the jeep rolled on past the dull tapping of a diesel generator towards the frontier post.

Local conditions mean that this building must be dug deep into the hillside, making it cool in summer and warm in winter. It provides all the usual comforts – hot baths, excellent freshly baked bread, Moscow television programmes picked up by satellite, and films and letters brought in by helicopter. The only thing they're short of here is water, and a woman has to make several trips down to the well every day to bring it up. But water is always a problem in these parts.

I jumped excitedly out of the car, shook hands with the tired Political Education Officer, and asked him how far the patrol had gone.

'To the first drop,' he said, jabbing his finger at the map in his room.

'Could we follow them?' I asked casually.

He glanced despairingly at our grinning escort. 'Not a chance. This is no place for outsiders.'

'How about the fortress, then?' I suggested.

He agreed and we set off.

Cut off from the frontier post by a shallow gorge, this fortress is in fact the ruined site of an ancient town, dating from between the thirteenth and the fifteenth centuries.

We slithered down the rocks, then scrambled up some steps cut into the cliff face and emerged at the ruins. In the gathering dusk this vast ravine of cracked and folded rocks looked like some eerie monolith. Far away to the east, beyond the desolate emptiness of the ravine, loomed the sheer wall of the Zulfaqar ridge, crimson in the last rays of the setting sun. The nearby slopes were scattered with the gravestones of ancient cemeteries. The distant outline of the frontier watchtower was visible through the damaged dome of the mosque at the edge of the ravine. Only the hovering silhouette of an eagle, stretched out high in the sky above us, broke the deathly stillness of the landscape.

'So where's their path?' I asked at last.

'Down there,' he said, kicking a stone into the gorge with the toe of his boot. 'They even took a motorbike down once. They're not going that way now, though. They're going over the ridge and along the river. We'll show you tomorrow.'

He adjusted his rifle and we retraced our steps. It was that fleeting moment of the day when sky and earth become one. At that very moment the night patrol were reaching the final stage of their route, the 'first drop' . . .

There is a triangular area on the map, topped by the southernmost point of the Soviet Union, Kushka. To the left, near the famous Badkhyz nature reserve, is the meeting-point of the three adjacent states. This meeting-point is known in laconic frontier slang as the 'junction'.

In these desolate places people are continually being arrested for straying over the frontier. Most are merely petty offenders, peasants accidentally wandering across in search of straying cattle, or hoodlums deliberately driving their scraggy cows on to the protected pastures of the nature reserve.

Smugglers, however, are another matter.

For everyone involved in this trade, Afghanistan is heaven on earth. The chaos and carnage of war have made it impossible to guard the frontiers, which have acquired an increasingly speculative character. Mujahedin from Iran and Pakistan now hop across them with the greatest of ease, and it's even easier for groups of smugglers, since drugs and light weapons are obviously simpler to transport than land-mines or rocket launchers. There's a constant traffic of guns from Iran into Afghanistan, where they are bartered for loads of heroin and raw opium, known locally as 'teryak'. (Drugs may be bought with any currency except roubles.)

The route back to Iran is more hazardous, since Ayatollah Khomeini has ordered the Islamic Revolutionary Guards and border police to shoot all drug smugglers on sight. This is why drugs are literally worth their weight in gold in Iran, and why so many smugglers stray over on to Soviet territory.

Their path hugs the line of the frontier, and their route is very simple. If they come across our patrols they cross over into neighbouring Iran, and if they meet the police there they run back over to our side. No ravine is too perilous for them, for the stakes are high in the drugs game.

Frontier guards have arrested numerous groups of drug smugglers over the past few years, and the landscape is littered with names like Novikov Point, or Dolgov Path, commemorating some of their more spectacular successes. I spoke to some members of the patrol before they set off again.

During his years on the southern frontier Captain Anatoly Konev has seized about a ton of heroin and raw opium, and was involved in a major raid last summer which yielded twenty machine-gun cartridges, twenty-two pistol cartridges, and over 257 kilograms of opium.

I asked Konev what they did with the drugs seized.

'The heroin we destroy,' he said, 'while the opium goes to make drugs, mainly psychiatric ones. A huge haul was recently seized near Ashkhabad and taken in an armoured car under armed guard to the airport, from where it was sent on to a pharmaceutical factory.'

But the main problem facing Konev and his colleagues is the tribes living close to our frontiers whose entire livelihood depends on drug-smuggling. The most successful of these are the Beludzhi tribes, who have emigrated from Afghanistan into Iran, 10,000 of whom now live in Afghanistan's Herat province.

'We have soldiers on duty here day and night,' said Major Nikolai Bychkov, who has recently taken over as head of the frontier post. 'Sometimes we just crash on to the ground where we are, sleep there all night if nothing happens, and climb the ridge back to the checkpoint next morning.

'I found it really hard here at first, because I'd had no special training. I couldn't believe it when I first saw the "second drop". It's just an invisible crevice in a sheer wall, but the soldiers ran down it without turning a hair, and now I've got the measure of the place too.'

'We always prepare for Islamic holidays much as we do for our own,' Konev told me. 'In three weeks' time, on 21 March, Muslims will be celebrating Novruz Bairam, their New Year. They're always in a mad rush beforehand. The main thing here is the shortages. The food situation is really dire in these border areas, but the first thing to run out is always drugs. Everyone around here either uses the stuff or trades in it.

'This time two years ago all the Iranian villages around here were completely deserted, and we eventually realised that almost the entire population had decamped into the interior of Iran to sell or consume drugs. So the day before yesterday, when the patrol reported that five armed youths had been seen crossing the "junction" from Iran into Afghanistan, we realised that it wouldn't be long before they were back.

'It was plain as daylight that they were smugglers. Firstly because they were armed. These lads often know more about firearms than us professionals, and they can shoot any target – a noise, a reflection, a rustle – although they try to use their weapons only when they're in a corner. The second thing about them is their gear. Most of the peasants around here have been resettled, and those who've stayed behind are desperately poor. Just a turban, a long shirt, and shoes if Allah wills it. The smuggling fraternity has left all that behind. Very smart those five lads looked yesterday, in their American "GI" camouflage shirts and brand-new Western jeans.

'According to our calculations, they'll be making their first trip back from the "junction" tonight, which means there's a good chance they'll hop back over to us in the morning. So at eight o'clock this evening we'll spread out in the undergrowth along the shore, fifty yards from the Iranian frontier.'

At eight that evening we stepped out of the frontier post for some fresh air. Darkness had fallen within about twenty minutes, bringing a cool breeze to the plateau and scattering stars across a velvet-black sky.

By then the night patrol was successfully negotiating the drop from the ridge towards the river, and discreetly stretching out along the shore to keep watch on the bend in the river. An hour and a half later, Captain Konev saw through his night binoculars the silhouette of an armed man moving along the other side of the river from the Afghan side of the 'junction'. The man crept along the riverbank scanning the Soviet side of the frontier.

'Although I'd been expecting to see someone it was still a shock when he appeared,' Konev told me later. 'Through my night binoculars I glimpsed the flash of a gun on his shoulder. When he turned round, I saw it was a machine-gun, and I knew he wouldn't hesitate to use it if he or his companions tried to cross the frontier.

'The man had evidently been sent on ahead to reconnoitre. He looked fit and well-built, but we have a tough team too, and we were ready for him. Two minutes later two more men appeared, one of them carrying a rifle. They stood opposite us, just twenty yards away, and started discussing what to do next, while the "scout" strode off down the river again, continually glancing over to our side. After walking for about half a mile, he turned back, evidently satisfied that all was quiet on our side. Then they all strolled out as relaxed as guests at a party, waving their arms and shouting in the direction they'd come from.

'At this point a whole caravan of them appeared. There were two armed men on foot leading five mules, and seated on the fifth mule was an old man who was evidently a local guide. The mules were loaded on each side with large panniers, and I could see with my night binoculars that they contained a considerable load. If it was raw opium, it must have weighed at least 900 kilograms. We haven't had a haul like that since last June.

'The five men gathered at the shore and started to discuss something. The old man didn't get off his mule. Then one of them made for the river and waded in, as though to test the crossing.

'It was still early spring and the water was cold. He hesitated for a second, then braced himself and struck out towards us. He only went as far as the middle, evidently knowing exactly where the line of the frontier was, then he stood up, screwing up his eyes like a cat. But you can't afford to mess around when you're carrying a load like that. They were heavily armed and loaded with drugs, and we knew they wouldn't hesitate to use their rifles on us.'

'The man in the river swam back to the shore, where the others were waiting for him,' said Major Bychkov, taking up the story. 'It seemed as though they were all going to cross the river. I turned round and nodded at Anatoly to confirm that we were ready.

'The "scout" had meanwhile rejoined the others, who were evidently weighing up the pros and cons of crossing the river. Then suddenly they all turned their backs on us and moved towards the frontier with Iran! They'd probably decided not to cross the river for fear of dropping their load, for the current was quite fast.

'Konev and I looked at each other in horror and threw up our arms. We tracked them on our side of the river, but they moved away from the frontier without a backward glance . . .'

It was a moonlit March night, and there was a restless breeze in the air. I followed the Political Education Officer outside. The beam of a searchlight licked the distant folds of the ridge, bathing them in a sinister deathly blue.

Towards dawn the night patrol returned. Maybe they'd be lucky next time.

'These customers don't give up that easily,' grinned the Political Education Officer. 'They've been at it for too long and the stakes are too high. Can you see that notch in the rock over there?' He waved his arm into the distance.

I could just make out a tiny white point on the moonlit rock face.

'We call that the Devil's Finger,' he said. 'It's a little pyramid of stones to show them the path, like a way-marker. When we first discovered them we used to knock them down, but they would pop up again, bang up against the frontier. So that means they're still going that way . . .'

The Political Education Officer went inside, shaking his head, and buried himself in his papers.

The moon hid behind a cloud, and we went to bed to the sounds of the wind banging against the window-sash. The frontier post slept.

Ashkhabad–Moscow

From documents of the trial of June 1987
Captain Konev's Testimony:
'At 13.55 hours on 1 June, the head of the border patrol observation group reported that three unknown men had been seen on Soviet territory, leading three horses and moving towards the point where the frontiers of the USSR, Iran, and Afghanistan join . . .'

From documents of the trial of 1987
Testimony of Alexander Vladimirovich Kourov:
'At 13.45 hours on 1 June 1987, my patrol arrived at the "second drop". I assigned the border patrol their observation posts and mounted guard.

'At 13.49 hours, Private Kovalchuk observed three men on Soviet territory leading three horses thirty yards from the river. They moved twenty yards along the sandy slope towards the "join", then two of them ducked into the bushes and brought out some white packages, which they placed in white panniers hanging on the horses. They unsaddled the horses, and two of them went down to the river for water, and brought some back to the third man. One had a machine-gun and all were masked . . .

'At 18.10 hours one of our helicopters appeared over the forested area on the right bank of the river and co-ordinated our movements.

'Abandoning their horses, the three men ran in different directions through the undergrowth. One then jumped out on to the sandy riverbank and ran over into Iranian territory. Higher upstream a second man jumped out . . .'

Testimony of Garry Borisovich Gerzhbak:
'Shchukin walked on. Then we heard him shout "Halt, or I'll shoot!" and fire a warning shot into the air. Korobov and I skirted the bend in the river to see one of the trespassers running on to the steep bank, jumping into the water, and swimming quickly across to the spit on the other side. I opened fire over his head, but he didn't react. Then I fired straight at the lower part of his body. He swerved to one side, but went on swimming towards the spit . . .'

Senior investigator Ataev has established:
'That on 1 June 1987 three unknown trespassers were discovered in

the vicinity of the frontier post. One was killed, and two others managed to escape into Iran. The trespassers' personal effects were removed, but along with Iranian border authorities, revolutionary guards and inhabitants of the nearby Iranian villages failed to identify the dead man, whose body was buried on Soviet territory . . .'

Expert witness's report:
'Forty samples of the dark brown substance presented at the investigation have proved to be the narcotic opium.

Signed: Z. E. Kaminskaya.'

The Square of Suffering
Special correspondent
Zamira Ibrahimova

At school we learned that our workers no longer had any reason to strike. They owned the factories and governed the country, and the dictatorship of the proletariat was the fairest system in the world.

Then in July 1989 the old museum images suddenly sprang back to life in Siberia's Kuznetsk coalfields. Thousands of miners came out on strike, demonstrating and sleeping on the town squares, forming strike committees, and refusing to return to the coal-face until their demands were met. The situation grew so explosive that the newspapers could hardly keep up. Leisurely historical assessments gave way to stark headlines such as 'Crisis at the pits', 'The strike continues', 'Negotiations have started'. And amazed journalists reported back in a state of shock from the seething squares: 'There are hundreds of Communists out there!'

The era of illusions is over. We can weep for our dreams of universal prosperity, but these vast strikes have robbed them for ever of their old anodyne function, and Prokopyevsk's Victory Square now echoes with the sounds of universal despair.

This is what the miners on the Square of Suffering are crying:

'Tell the world we're treated like dirt! Down the pits and on the surface!'

'Prices are going up and wages are going down!'

'How can we help the developing countries when we're under-developed ourselves!'

'Yesterday we were given rotten sausage – we gave it to the boss!'

'We get fifteen roubles a shift. We live on credit – we don't make money, we work to pay it back!'

'My wife earns more than I do. Should I change my wife or change my job?'

'A mining economist gets 700 roubles a month, and a miner gets just 200 to 300. Where's the justice in that?'

'The drillers need more holiday, else we won't be off till autumn!'

'They're saving on rubber so our boots collapse after a day, and we're supposed to make them last six months!'

'Marx said heavy labour makes people drink.'

'That's why we got all the drink shops closed down. The bosses wanted us drunk, but we weren't falling for it!'

'We're not against the Soviet authorities. The local people have done all they could for us!'

'We've no faith in them! Send us Gorbachev. He'd have something to offer us.'

'The others keep promising us things, but they've no authority.'

'All industries should be made independent!'

'Support Yeltsin!'

'Keep politics out of it. This is an economic strike!'

'But the government's responsible. We kept sending them telegrams!'

'But our phones were cut and our microphones disconnected . . . !'

So what are the miners fighting for? Their answers are very simple.

'We want decent wages!'

'And extra pay for dangerous conditions!'

'We want to start our shift on a full stomach!'

'And running water in our homes!'

Anyone who knows anything about the miners' lives will support their demands.

The Prokopyevsk–Kiselev region of the Kuznetsk coalfields contains some of the most geologically complex coalmines in the Soviet Union, and some of its most primitive working and living conditions. All the mines here date from the war, if not before, and the work of renovating them has been extremely slow. 'This is like the Dark Ages!' said some American journalists after going down the pits during the strike and seeing the machinery, most of which dates from the 1930s. And the strikers happily passed on their remark as though it justified all those days out of work.

Dozens of wretched settlements cluster around the mines. Uncomfortable, unhygienic, and hopelessly dilapidated, they are a living record of the miners' lives during the first Five-year plans and the years before and after the war. The people living in these hovels will laugh angrily when economists explain that a ton of coal mined in the Kuznetsk fields and taken to Moscow will cost less than the same weight mined and sold in the Ukrainian Donbass. If the Siberian ton costs less, it is at the expense of slums instead of proper homes, streets full of rubbish, unbuilt roads, kindergartens, and hospitals, and exhausted mines created at the height of the war, when the miners rescued the country in its most difficult hour. In the fifth decade of peace the Kuznetsk miners are still stranded at this level of poverty.

To those who mine it, the costs of this 'cheap' Kuznetsk coal are enormous in terms of workplace injuries, industrial illnesses, and premature death. During the strike, local newspapers printed information which was seized upon by those in the square: 'Some 15,000 Soviet soldiers died in nine days in Afghanistan. In nine days in the Soviet Union we lost 10,000 men in the mines. One death for every million tons of coal. Last year 152 miners died in the Kuznetsk fields . . .'

Everyone at these demonstrations knows that the various worthy resolutions adopted throughout the years here have had virtually no effect. The introduction of tariffs, which they see as behind the sudden reduction in their wages, is not new either. Nor is the deteriorating industrial situation, nor the housing crisis.

So what was it that so enraged the sober miners in the hot July of 1989?

'It's a soap riot! I need a whole bar of it after a shift!' said one.

He was sharply interrupted by another: 'Don't cheapen our strike! We're not selling ourselves for a bit of soap or meat. We're tired of waiting and hoping, but we don't need bribes. We need a living wage.'

The miners have intuitively sensed the possibility of improvement in the new economic thinking, even though the term 'regional self-financing' is one they find hard to understand. This is hardly surprising, given our present muddled financing methods.

Take the Kemerovo region, with its huge metallurgical, chemical, and mining industries, which for years has been living on credit and buying more than it sells. The mystery is explained by comparing the price of coal in the Soviet Union – fourteen roubles a ton – with the forty-two dollars it would fetch on the world market.

Can the Kuznetsk fields still provide the 'cheapest' coal under self-financing without overpricing it? This is not something the miners on the square can answer, but their demonstrations have at least posed the question.

After years spent fruitlessly petitioning local leaders and Siberian scientists, it's not surprising that the miners have finally run out of patience. 'There's no doubting the justice of their strike, and we've done them a great wrong by not getting Moscow to listen to our problems before,' says the director of the Prokopyevsk hydrocoal plant. 'Yet it's doing us enormous financial damage.'

He handed me a sheet of paper listing the losses ensuing from just twenty-four hours' lost work. These amount to 1,376,000 roubles, the equivalent to a 150-apartment building. The strikers have thus wasted seven such buildings – which wouldn't be built, of course, because the region is catastrophically short of builders and building materials.

What they have gained, however, is the unique experience of articulating their needs. The president of the regional strike committee, People's Deputy Avaliani Teimuraz, told me:

'The strike has shown how uneducated we still are. We came out first, *then* started working out our demands. Or take a recent strike meeting in the main square in Kiselevsk. A woman came up and spoke passionately in support of issuing coupons for sausage; it would be fair, she said, and would hurt no one. People voted, and almost the whole square were in favour, with only 200 against. Then another woman came up and argued just as passionately that we had just made a huge political mistake, and that if coupons were introduced we'd never get rid of them, and soon all our food would be rationed. So people voted again, and this time almost everyone supported her, with only 300 against.

'We haven't been trained to operate politically, and it has been a great problem for us. The strike started on the 11th, but it wasn't until the 16th that we elected a strike committee. We tried to summarise the demands of the various different towns, but each of them raised dozens of issues, from the most general, such as banning censorship in the media, to the most local: roads, hospitals, schools, and so on. A special government commission will soon be arriving, and I shall have only three typewritten pages to show them, containing less than half of our total demands. We should learn the rules of striking, and how to conduct them properly. And of course we're nowhere near being able to talk seriously about regional self-financing, although we shall ask the Siberian Academy of Sciences to help us . . .'

The people standing on the squares anxiously await the latest bulletin from the negotiations. Banners announce: 'Comrade miners, we are with you! The Miner's Wife Clothes Factory.' 'Solidarity with the striking miners! We have collected 50,000 roubles for your strike fund.' Since the striking towns' telephone lines have been cut, messengers travel to and fro, excitedly explaining what they want and what they won't give in on.

The police share their lunch with the miners. 'We made contact with the strike committee and offered to help them keep order,' said the deputy head of Prokopyevsk's police force. 'We were with them right from the start. We knew that this was an economic strike and there was no politics in it, and no fear of the banditry we saw in Sumgait or Karabakh.'

The miners constantly contrast the image of that vicious and unnecessary slaughter with what is happening in the coalfields.

Workers throughout the region wanted to join the strikers. But they would only accept tokens of solidarity, and appealed instead for contributions to their strike funds. 'All the factories here wanted to come out in support of us, but it would have done us no good if they had,' says Alexei Ipatenko, a member of the Kemerovo strike committee. 'So we went round the factories and talked to them, and they understood. We don't want another Karabakh here!'

The endless wait on the squares finally ends with the announcement on the radio of a thirty-five-point plan, signed by members of the government commission and the strike committee. These points include increased pay for evening and night shifts; various additional social payments; the immediate provision of extra food supplies, clothing, and household goods; full economic and legal independence for all local enterprises, with regional self-financing to be introduced on 1 January 1990.

'The strike committees will exist until 1 August 1989,' says Point 31. 'The question of their further existence will be decided in the light of events.'

Those July days gave birth to a dynamic new structure of workers' self-management. The unions, on the other hand, found no place for themselves in the strike. When addressing the striking miners in Prokopyevsk for the last time, the president of their strike committee said: 'Do we believe in our committees? Or will the union crush us?

See what a mighty bureaucratic machine they have, with all their staff and their printing-presses, and yet how toothless they are! Our strike committees will be a worthy alternative to them!'

Most miners don't have much good to say about the unions. But when structures have outlived their usefulness life itself always finds something to replace them, and the strike produced large numbers of bright, resourceful people who should go far under the new set-up.

The Kuznetsk miners were supported by miners all over the country. Yet the main purpose of their strike was not to improve the economic crisis in our country, but to enable people to express their own needs. There is no other way. Kuznetsk's squares of suffering have forced the Supreme Soviet to turn its attention to miners throughout the country, and they have the power to satisfy many of their demands. The strikers have been heard. There is hope.

What Price Sobriety?
Lev Miroshnichenko

The time has come to reassess our desperate three-year battle against alcohol. Every conceivable weapon has been used, and in May 1985 a draconian new anti-alcohol law was introduced. Yet the old enemy is still going strong.

There have been some hopeful signs. In 1984 the Soviet population bought and consumed over 3 billion gallons of alcohol, whereas in 1987 the flow had been reduced to just under 2 billion. Drunken absenteeism and workplace injuries are down.

So why not simply go on fighting the enemy in the same way?

Alas, it is becoming increasingly evident that the successes have been modest, to say the least, and have actually produced a whole variety of unpleasant new problems.

Even though the price of vodka has doubled, reduced sales over the past three years have lost the treasury 37 billion roubles. Such financial losses would be justified in a good cause, but cold statistics show that we're drinking roughly as much now as we did in 1985. Vodka sales have fallen from 2.5 to 1.2 billion litres, but sugar sales have leapt to 1.5 billion kilograms, and this amply covers the government's losses on alcohol. Many towns are even issuing people with sugar ration-cards, as in wartime, so presumably we shall soon be seeing shortages of sweets, toffees, fruit juice, and jam too.

It is indeed a war to the death. The enemy has suffered grave losses, yet its ranks have been barely dented. Eighty thousand illegal distillers were caught in 1985, 150,000 in 1986, and 397,000 in 1987. Two hundred and seventy thousand people fell into the net in just the first five months of this year, and 2.7 million were arrested on alcohol-related offences.

Police use sniffer-dogs to track down illegal stills, and organise large-scale raids on houses and flats which often come dangerously

close to violating the constitutional inviolability of the home. There were a number of such raids recently in villages in the Kursk, Tomsk, and Kharkov areas, and home-brewed beer and vodka was discovered in every third or fourth house.

Although the Ministry of Internal Affairs has hailed all this as a great triumph, it somehow fails to bring one much pleasure, and increasing numbers of people continue to risk imprisonment and confiscation of property. The distillers go to unbelievable lengths, making stills out of milling machines, hiding their hooch in attics, barns, and hayricks, burying it in the vegetable patch and even the manure heap, and setting up shop in offices, workshops, and factories.

Even though home-brew is much more toxic, it's in great demand, hence its price: up to seventy roubles for a three-litre bottle. It's not surprising it's so expensive, and you'll pay an arm and a leg for the stuff if you do manage to get hold of it in the shops.

In Petrozavodsk, all the drink shops are patrolled by military-style detachments of ten policemen. But even these have proved ineffective. Just before New Year, a crowd of five thousand people pushed back a lorry and smashed down the door of a wine shop, and an old woman battling for refreshments for her visiting relatives was crushed to death against the doorpost.

Shop assistants, taxi-drivers, lavatory attendants, and railway conductors all speculate in spirits, and a highly organised alcohol mafia is emerging. Meanwhile the police are too busy dashing between the profiteers, the distillers, and the wineshop queues to follow up domestic burglaries, which are consequently on the increase.

Drinkers raid the shops and chemists for eau-de-cologne, hair lotion, varnish, embrocation, window-cleaning liquid, and mouth-wash. People simply cannot buy cheap, basic alcohol solutions any more, and nurses have nothing with which to wipe patients' buttocks before an injection.

But these alcohol substitutes exact a far higher toll, in terms of human lives, and many cases involve whole groups of people at home or work. Eleven thousand people were killed in this way last year, almost as many as the Soviet troops killed in Afghanistan. In one recent case, the director of a village school in the Ukraine gave a farm mechanic a drink for moving some furniture. The next morning the mechanic died. He was followed a couple of days later by the director. The same alcohol substitute was served at the director's funeral, and eight more people, including the mechanic's daughter and two sons, followed the director to the grave.

Various things were overlooked at the start of this holy war, targeted as it is on alcohol itself and those who drink, rather than the causes driving them to do so. It was hoped that limiting people's access to spirits would have a healthy effect on a new generation of children. But in fact adolescent crime is on the increase, and half a million teenagers are now on the files of the Ministry of Internal Affairs' juvenile crime department.

A survey has revealed that 80 per cent of the adult population consumes just as much alcohol as before, and fewer people have joined the abstinence brigade than the campaign's enthusiasts had at first hoped.

We must achieve our perestroika not with the 20 per cent who are teetotallers, but with the 80 per cent who drink. Alcohol consumption in this country has rocketed over the last twenty years. People started drinking openly and arriving drunk for work, and the number of industrial injuries and other drink-related evils shot up. Yet to any thoughtful observer it was obvious even then that the cause of these evils went far deeper than the mere availability of alcohol. We have been tackling only the consequences, for the causes until recently couldn't be openly discussed.

Now, however, the causes can be spelt out. As the journalist Nikolai Shmelyov writes: 'The main reason drunkenness increased between the sixties and the eighties is that people were tired of muddle and dishonesty, and of having nothing to which to apply their hand or brain.'

Yet we go on tackling the alcohol problem with methods more appropriate to the stagnant sixties and seventies than to the revolutionary transformations of the eighties. Before launching this campaign, it might have been wise to ask a few hard questions.

Why, for instance, if people in Brazil can buy a tank of cheap rum at any time of the day or night to fill up their cars, are the streets not littered with drunks?

Why in Soviet Georgia or Armenia, where the hillsides are smothered in vineyards and every peasant has at least two barrels of wine in the cellar, are there seven to ten times fewer alcoholics than in Russia? And why are the sobering-up cells in Tbilisi and Erevan empty?

Why has Japan recently introduced 170,000 twenty-four-hour alcohol vending machines, thus enabling the entire adult population to drink themselves permanently blotto?

Why has alcohol consumption steadily dropped off of its own accord in most of the developed countries, where wine is still cheap and freely available?

Why do we have to be forced to adopt a 'healthy life', and why do people here generally regard it as a bugbear?

Unfortunately the desire to finish off the problem in one mighty administrative swoop has taken the upper hand. It was hoped to recruit millions of volunteers into the new Temperance Society. But this proved a typically grandiose bureaucratic structure into which 'volunteers' had to be enlisted by force.

The society has roughly 450,000 local branches, littering the country from the tropics to the Arctic. These local branches are answerable to over 3,000 'higher bodies' in the districts and towns, which in turn take their orders from the next level in the temperance hierarchy, at provincial, regional, and republic level. Reigning supreme in the temperance firmament, in a red-columned building in the capital itself, sits the Central Temperance Society, complete with president, vice-presidents, secretary, administrators, and a vast staff of officials. The Society employs six and a half thousand state employees, all paid for by its 15 million rank-and-file members, who each contribute one rouble, and the government also provides a hefty grant. The 164,000 members of the Society's 'soviets' are paid by their employers to take time off work to attend regular meetings, at which they discuss, approve, and encourage the Society's work.

It's hardly surprising, therefore, that this huge hierarchical organisation has proved so ineffective. For all its noise and thunder, it benefits no one but itself, and it is common knowledge that over a third of its members are heavy drinkers, that branch presidents regularly spend the night in the sobering-up cells, and that people have to be dragooned into the anti-alcohol lectures in the factories.

Some people do join the Society with the sincere desire to do good, but they have little clout, and most of the Society's public pronouncements consist of appeals to drive yet more drinkers into the corner. One leading member, writing recently in the magazine *Temperance and Culture*, expressed the view that police tracking down alcohol heretics should be able to break into houses without a search warrant from the local prosecutor, and that society members should have the power to fine drunkards.

Finding so little support from the ordinary population, society activists have now made common cause with various local officials who warm to their old-fashioned campaigning style. Hence all those villages and districts which were proclaimed 'temperance zones', an experiment which quietly collapsed in ignominy. Hence all those sham alcohol-free weddings, with a policeman at the door and vodka in the samovars. Hence the demented frenzy with which the authorities in Azerbaijan, Georgia, Moldavia, and the Crimea ploughed up thousands of acres of magnificent vineyards, even though the country consumes only ten pounds of grapes per person every year.

The summer before last, I visited the laboratory of an analyst friend and colleague, and was surprised to see not the usual blood samples, but an expensive computer-powered chromatograph surrounded by a battery of bottles and jars containing clotted cream, buttermilk, and fruit juices.

'I've been given a special government assignment to analyse the alcohol content of this lot,' he explained.

'And have you found much?'

'It varies, but you find the damned stuff wherever you look. A litre of juice contains five to six grams, buttermilk eight to ten grams, kvass* between twelve and fifteen. So instead of drinking thirty grams of vodka you could quietly put away a litre of kvass.'

This ludicrous all-out war against buttermilk is being waged by extremists from the Society who have been trying to convince us that babies are being 'addicted to alcohol' at the breast, and have spent the past two years petitioning the Ministry of Health, the Soviet of Ministers, and the Party Central Committee for it to be banned.

One of the chief mistakes of all our recent anti-alcohol campaigns has been to confuse normal drinking with alcoholism.

Only Islamic states like Iran, Turkey, Malaysia, and Pakistan campaign against alcohol. Why should they be our examples? None of the developed countries campaign against drinking itself, but try on the contrary to provide as pleasant conditions as possible for its consumption. Tokyo, for instance, has 3,000 bars, restaurants, night-clubs, cafés, and snack-bars offering a huge variety of drinks. Revellers in Moscow have a choice of 3,000 cosy slums and sewers.

*A popular soft drink made from fermented bread.

The crude logic here is that fewer bars mean fewer drunks. But this rule, born in some bureaucrat's brain, bears little relation to the reality in Moscow, where the last bar was closed down long ago, but where last year 330,000 people – almost a thousand every day – ended up in the sobering-up cell.

Why can't we admit that the law of May 1985 was one-sided and unworkable? There have been so many similar laws recently, involving so much wasted time, energy, and money, so much economic and moral damage.

We have conveniently forgotten the law of 1972 'On measures to strengthen the battle against drunkenness and alcoholism'. Yet this law contained virtually everything that was in the bill of May 1985: alcohol production was reduced, heavy fines were imposed on drunkards, conniving bosses, illegal distillers, speculators, and drunken drivers; and all this punishment and compulsion went under the slogan of 'developing cultural and educational work'.

The 1972 bill was carried out with a great deal of administrative zeal and publicity. Supported by local party leaders and administrators, thousands of temperance commissions were established up and down the country, millions of lectures were delivered, papers issued, and plans and schemes drawn up. Yet it ran out of steam almost immediately, and was soon hopelessly bogged down in bureaucracy. It was just fortunate that they hadn't time to run their bulldozers through the vineyards.

Those were the days of phoney success, official secrecy, and bureaucratic insanity. But what's to stop us now from going to the real heart of the problem? Why not admit that the law of May 1985 was drawn up in the spirit of the recent 'stagnation era', before the new thinking of perestroika could be reflected in it?

We appear to have lost the latest anti-alcohol campaign, and we risk grave danger if the present crude policies continue. By May 1988, the country had already consumed its entire twelve-month sugar reserves, and to alleviate the 'sugar crisis' the Ministry of Trade will have to buy an additional 800,000 tons from abroad, at a cost of billions of dollars. And this in the highest sugar-producing country in the world!

And how are we to assess the damaged morale of the 160 million people persecuted for liking a drink? Doesn't their antagonism also hinder the progress of perestroika?

We have to change tack.

The humiliating queues outside the drink shop must go. Alcohol must be priced low enough to ensure that people are deterred from home-brewing by its health risks, the danger of being caught, and its general amorality, while high enough to ensure that sugar consumption falls to 1.5 million tons.

The All-Union Temperance Society, which discredits the humane motives of those who genuinely care about the problem, must have its apparatus reduced, while local branches must be decentralised and made genuinely voluntary.

Anti-alcohol propaganda must be purged of all 'salutary lies'. Propagandists have got away for too long with the most ludicrous statements in their desire to frighten people off alcohol. This sort of dishonest mass propaganda provokes apathy and outright hostility, and is the cause of innumerable personal tragedies and millions of wasted roubles and man-hours.

Alcoholism must be properly recognised as an illness. Alcoholic patients must not be used as cheap labour in the factories under the guise of 'work therapy'. Paid sick-leave for alcoholics undergoing treatment, abolished in 1972, must be restored.

The question of how and when to give up alcohol is one that we must all decide together, drinkers and non-drinkers alike, without mistrust or recriminations. We must allow plenty of open arguments, and the citizens of Russia and the Ukraine must not impose their views on those of Georgia or Armenia, where attitudes to alcohol are very different. We may need a referendum on the issue, to be conducted separately in each republic.

Meanwhile the population has voted instinctively on the issue, with endless queues for drink and oceans of home-brew.

P.S. It has just come to our attention that the authorities in Kiev have voted to declare the capital of the Ukraine an alcohol-free town next year. How simple! Pass a resolution and there's an end to it. How many lives, how many millions of roubles, will this absurd administrative experiment cost?

Interview with an Anti-Hero
Dmitry Gubin

A Soviet citizen in Leningrad takes desperate measures to expose the violent, quasi-fascistic Pamyat group, whose activities are reminiscent of the anti-Semitic louts of the Black Hundred gangs before the revolution.

On 18 September 1988 Arkady Norinsky, forty-two years old and with no previous convictions, was found guilty by the Vasilev Island People's Court of sending dozens of threatening anonymous letters throughout the summer to leading politicians, signed 'Fighters of the Patriotic Pamyat Organisation'.

'I wanted to bring Pamyat's activities to the attention of the authorities, and to force them to ban it,' Norinsky said in court, where he was sentenced to eighteen months' probation for 'hooliganism'.

Jewish, unmarried, and a non-party member, Norinsky is a strange, rather solitary man, who works as a stoker. Journalists' views of the case varied widely, and I was unsure how to react to him when he rushed towards me outside the district court building. His eyes were small, dark, and lively, and he seemed to speak rather incoherently, waving his arms and constantly returning to the same subject.

But afterwards, when I played back my tape of our conversation, I realised that he spoke with amazing clarity and conviction.

'It's Pamyat that's guilty of hooliganism, not me. Guilty not only of hooliganism either, but of slander, insulting behaviour, and inciting racial hatred. If a man insults me in the market I don't complain. If someone hates the Jews or some other race that's their business. But when I see the Leningrad Pamyat group peddling anti-Semitism, and a placid policeman laughing as he reads one of their Gestapo-style leaflets, I ask myself what has happened to Article 74 of our Criminal

Code, which is supposed to outlaw this kind of racist propaganda. So I decided to get Pamyat banned myself. For me it was simply a matter of self-defence, as though someone had insulted my mother . . .

'I'm not a Zionist – what do I know about Israel? All my relatives fought for Soviet power, and my grandfather was even awarded a watch "For sterling defence of the proletarian revolution". My father was an engineer in a factory, whose family was shot by the Gestapo in Krasnodar, and my mother was a shop assistant whose relatives were either killed in pogroms in the Ukraine in 1910, or died in the Nazis' gas chambers. As a citizen of the Soviet state, I can at least demand that its courts defend my good name and that of my mother and my relatives . . .'

What was Norinsky's evidence that Pamyat was inciting racial hatred?

'I just used to go to work and come home again, and never asked myself if there was a "Jewish question" – or if I did, it never bothered me, and I never encountered any discrimination at work.

'Before coming to Leningrad I worked in the Tomsk area in Siberia, where I made friends with an interesting chap called Ozhegin, who was captain of a detachment in a camp – and I don't mean a holiday camp. In March this Ozhegin visited Leningrad, and said: "This time I've brought you something more interesting than a bag of nuts!" And he handed me some leaflets signed "Pamyat". This was at the time when the Democratic Unions, Informals, and all sorts of other unofficial Leningrad political groups were meeting outside the Kazan Cathedral. I'd heard the press attacking Pamyat, of course, but I'd always assumed it was just propaganda. Anyway I read these leaflets for myself and said to Ozhegin: "Looks like you'll soon be having some intelligent people in your camp instead of yobs . . . !" Then off we went to the Kazan Cathedral.

'Some man was standing there telling everyone that the Jews were a nation of idiots. "What about Einstein?" someone called out from the crowd. "He just worked in the patent office and stole other people's ideas!" the man shouted back.

'Ozhegin then said: "You're as bad as the Black Hundreds!"

'And the man said: "But there are millions of us – we're the Black Millions . . . !"

'After that I began noticing Pamyat leaflets stuck up in Mikhailov

Park, which said that all meetings there were part of some Zionist plot. I couldn't really understand this, but to be honest I quite liked it. Some people can't stand the Jews, I reasoned, just as some people can't stand the Soviet government. Each to his own tastes – so what if they're anti-Semitic, at least they're sticking their necks out and speaking up.

'Apart from this, I had no further contact with Pamyat until three months later.

'One day in June or early July, I was making my way along the embankment to an exhibition at the Academy of Arts, and I saw lots of police in Rumyantsev Park, and someone addressing a huge crowd of about 500 people through a loud-hailer. I assumed they must be making a film. But as I got closer I heard the words "Union of the Russian People", and "Union of Michael the Archangel". These repulsive groups, which organised pogroms of the Jews before the revolution, were "humane organisations", explained the speaker, which were "deeply concerned about Russian history and committed to purge Russia of Zionism". They hadn't achieved everything, apparently, because of the "October Zionist revolution", in which the Jews had seized power, and the Sverdlovs, Uritskys, Trotskys, and Dzerzhinskys had sent Russia to the dogs . . .

'There then followed a long list of Jewish commanders and commissars who had destroyed Russia during the civil war. One of Pamyat's leaders – a man with a moustache called Lysenko – stood up and said: "Commissar of the Seventh Army?" Pause. "A *Jew*!" And the crowd roared. "Commissar of the Ninth Army? A *Jew*!" On and on he went. Then he got on to how many members of the Bolshevik government had been Jews – or Latvians. They hate the Latvians too for some reason, although not as much as the Jews.

'Having dealt with the war and the first Bolshevik government, they moved on to the famine in the Ukraine. Almost all my family came from the Ukraine; my mother very nearly died in the famine, and she used to tell me how the dying were thrown into the wells, and the railway stations were cordoned off by the NKVD . . . Well, the Jews were behind all that, of course.

'Then came the Second World War, in which the Zionists paid the fascists to spare all the rich Jews, so that only the poor ones were killed.

'After the war they dealt with Soviet cultural groups, which the Jews have apparently taken over. There aren't many Jews in our country, they said, but those there are have monopolised all the key positions – various statistics followed. The composer Andrei Petrov is a Jew, we were told, who has assumed a Russian name; the writer Baklanov is one too – real name such-and-such; the film director Svetozarov is one, and the son of the director Joseph Heifitz . . .

'Everywhere the Jews have seized power and turned Russia into a nation of alcoholics. They've cheated the Russians and destroyed their dignity. The Russians in Russia are now the most disenfranchised people in the world, worse off even than the blacks in South Africa . . .

'Then they started talking about Chernobyl . . .'

So the Jews were responsible for that too?

'Some speakers said they'd seen an article which appeared in a Novosibirsk newspaper ten days before the explosion, and had warned that all the Jews living in Chernobyl had left. There was a pentagram in the newspaper, they said, based on some idea of Madame Blavatsky's, and if you fiddled around with it you'd come up with the letters "Ch". I didn't really understand this, but the upshot was that Chernobyl was a Zionist provocation, in revenge for the way the Jews had been treated in the Ukraine.'

Could Norinsky describe some examples of Pamyat's propaganda?

'They slander the dead. In July, *Leningrad Pravda* published an obituary of Izaak Zaltsman, a former commissar and director of the Kirov armaments plant. Pamyat said: "Do you know the truth about this Jew? He was sentenced after the war for corrupting minors! We have our people working in the archives, and can find these things out!"

'An old man standing next to me said: "The swine! I knew Zaltsman since he was a lad, and he was a good man. He saved people from being arrested and gave them his rations . . ."

'Then at Pamyat meetings they get their supporters to mingle with the crowd like chance onlookers. One of them, a maths lecturer at the University whom I've seen at many Pamyat meetings, once casually approached a man next to me and said: "I have just come from a congress of mathematicians in Minsk, at which at least 95 per cent of those present were Jews."

' "So what?" said the man.

' "Why, mathematics means rockets, ballistic missiles, and so on . . ."

'A lot of their supporters are just cardsharpers, though, who get their cronies to sit beside them and win, so as to get other people to play and lose.

'Another thing about them is their mania for secret signs. Why is there no cross on the Kazan Cathedral, now the Museum of Religion and Atheism? Because "the Jews have turned it into a synagogue and removed the cross, so the Russian man can no longer pray . . ."

'I myself was baptised, and when I was a child in the Ukraine we lived near an Orthodox convent. But religious faith should be judged by what we do, and I have nothing in common with their kind of Christianity. It's a Christianity based on knowing the Psalter, and how many times to bow. There's no "love thy neighbour" in it, no compassion . . .'

What were the other objects of Pamyat's hatred?

'I remember one of their leaders attacking *Ogonyok* and saying that everyone holding a copy of it was holding the Star of David. He didn't like *Moscow News* either, or *Banner*, and the only magazine he said people should read was *Our Contemporary*. At this point a woman came running on to the platform and said: "There's only one way you can prove to us you're not Zionists, and that's to come right up and subscribe to *Our Contemporary*!"

'Then suddenly one of their favourite marching-songs came blaring out of ten loudspeakers:

> With thundering fire and glittering steel
> We set forth on our valiant campaign
> We who are summoned to battle by Stalin . . . and so on.

'People rushed up to subscribe to *Our Contemporary*, and spoke of the courage of its editor for daring to publish the novel *Judgement Day*. Pamyat supporters read *Our Contemporary* like a pornographer reads *Playboy* magazine.'

So how had Norinsky initially tried to alert the authorities to Pamyat's activities?

'It was hard to believe they didn't know anything. Everyone must have heard one of Pamyat's leaders shouting into a loudhailer at Rumyantsev Park that he wouldn't mind being shot if only a few more Jews were hanged. I actually knew the man – he used to be a director at Lenfilm, although all he ever did was to rant on about Heifitz, and he never made one film . . .

'The first Pamyat leaflets I read coincided with Nina Andreeva's article in *Soviet Russia*, demanding that Russia be "saved from glasnost and democracy". This article came out on 13 March, and the following week I wrote to *Soviet Russia* enclosing a Pamyat leaflet and suggesting that instead of publishing Andreeva's letter they'd do better to turn their attention to Pamyat. At the same time I wrote a letter to Vlasov, who was then Minister of Internal Affairs, and I signed it and put my address. I sent Vlasov the same leaflet, because although it's ostensibly about the "plots of international Zionism", it's really about what's going on here, which could easily lead to a nationalist bloodbath, as in Karabakh . . .

'I got no answer, either from Vlasov or from *Soviet Russia*. I'd written several short pieces in the past and sent them round to various papers, and if they didn't want something they'd always write back to say why. I've got stacks of these letters at home. But this time there was absolutely nothing. And that was that. It was then that I lost faith in the authorities. I decided I wasn't going to spend the rest of my life trying to drag an answer out of the minister, and I started writing letters in the name of Pamyat.'

I wondered if Norinsky had improvised these letters.

'I remember one of Pamyat's leaders shouting at a meeting: "Here are the names of those who will answer before the Russian people and the law!" The editor of *Moscow News* was to be arrested, and the editor of *Ogonyok*, and the General Secretary of the Communist Party, because all three were "Zionists". Then there was Academician Likhachev, for whom I have the greatest respect, and who merely called on Russian people to save old monuments, diverting their attention from the fact that their nation was being wiped out.

'"Vengeance will be ours!" the man screamed, waving around his list, which he was going to send to the Supreme Court. And I thought, very well, I'll tell all the people he's threatening what he said, and I wrote them all identical letters:

> We shall punish you!
> Fighters of the Pamyat patriotic organisation.
> VENGEANCE WILL BE OURS!

'The last sentence was in large letters so it would be the first thing they saw when they opened the envelope.

'I divided Leningrad into its various districts. The Kazan Cathedral, where Pamyat held its meetings, is in the Kuibishev district, and they hadn't touched them there. So I wrote to its district committee secretary, the police, and the local KGB. Rumyantsev Park comes under the Vasilev Island district committee, so I wrote to them too.

'I never imagined my letters would create such a panic, with district secretaries hiding under tables and Pamyat meetings being banned . . .'

Norinsky also wrote to the Dzerzhinsky Museum in Leningrad, saying they were going to be bombed.* This was rather hard to understand, since Dzerzhinsky is long dead and wasn't even Jewish.

'Pamyat says that both Dzerzhinsky and Bukharin were Jews who concealed their identity by using other names. I don't exactly worship Dzerzhinsky's memory, but the KGB has his portraits up on all the walls, so you'd think they'd have something to say about it!

'But anyone may be a secret Jew for them. Take your name. Why Gubin? It must be Gruber, or Gubelman. You must have something to hide!'

And why did he send those obscene letters to Victor Cherkesov, head of the investigation department of the Leningrad KGB?

'At the trial the investigator said: "This is pathological! A sane person doesn't send letters to the KGB!" But psychiatric tests showed I was quite normal.

'A lot of people in Pamyat are criminally insane, though. At least five of them are psychopaths. One of them is constantly handing out leaflets, but I'm not so worried about the ones who chatter away to satisfy their vanity. It's the really violent ones that frighten me. You

---

*Felix Dzerzhinsky (1877–1926), the Bolsheviks' first Commissar of Internal Affairs, organiser of the Vecheka, or secret police.

can see it in their eyes. There are a number of mad, hysterical women in Pamyat who walk around with huge folding icons. I once heard one of them say: "I slashed my wrists so I wouldn't have to look that vile race in the eyes."

'But I had good reason to write to Cherkesov.

'A few years ago I bumped into an Armenian fellow named Nazaryan. You could see at once that he was an unusual person. He told me that in Armenia there was an organisation fighting for the independence of the Armenian people. A lot of them had been sent to camps, he said, and the police were hard on his heels too, so he had to emigrate to America. "You're a Jew," he ended up. "You can help me get out." It was that kind of conversation, if you follow me.

'Some time later I was summoned to appear at the Department of State Security as a witness. I went, and there I met Victor Cherkesov, who asked me all about Nazaryan.

'"What's he done? Plotted a revolution?" I joked. And Cherkesov replied that he had incited racial hatred in Armenia, and that this was a very serious crime.

'"How can it be a crime?" I said. "They don't want to bring down the Soviet government or the army. They just want Armenia for the Armenians."

'And Cherkesov said: "There's a lot you don't understand. It starts with leaflets and goes on from there. Think of the Jewish pogroms, and the way the Armenians suffered under the Nazis . . ."

'I sat there while he gave me a two-hour pep talk on the evils of nationalism. He was angry, but he talked good sense . . .

'Then ten years later I switch on the television and see Victor Cherkesov holding forth as head of the investigation department of the Leningrad KGB about a huge smuggling network on the Baltic coast. So that's why I decided to write to him . . .'

Norinsky was discovered in record time. No sooner had he penned the last letter than he was sitting in court.

'When they caught me in Rumyantsev Park in August I was in such a state of elation that I started shouting: "It was me who did it . . . !"

'They then wrote to Pamyat saying they couldn't hold meetings for the time being, as the park needed repairs. A major in the police force came along and told everyone to clear off. Then one of the leaders ran out and said: "Men of Rus! This is a clear provocation! The Zionists have planned these so-called repairs to stop the Russian man from speaking, even though Mikhailov Park is now completely in their hands! More than 700 Zionists have written to us to complain. They are slanderers, and our weapon against them shall be the pen! We shall collect signatures to send to the regional committee and the KGB . . ." And they immediately started distributing petition forms.

'At this point a woman stepped out and spoke to the leaders, Riverov and Lysenko. "Honoured Yury, honoured Nikolai, I am a simple Russian woman. In 1920 the Jews massacred some peaceful eunuch monks in the Tver region, and this little icon is all they left. I bless you with this icon, and may you be victorious in battle." At this point Riverov knelt before her, as though receiving inspiration from her. The whole of Pamyat is like the last scene from Gogol's *The Inspector General*. The last scene in more ways than one, because after this Rumyantsev Park was closed down and everyone had to leave . . .'

How had Pamyat reacted to Norinsky's trial?

'Quite a lot of Pamyat people turned up in court, including a couple of their leaders. I tried to talk about their activities in court, and asked the investigator if I could bring in my own witnesses, but he kept interrupting me saying I was the one on trial. "But if someone commits a crime and isn't caught, he'll just do it again," I protested.

'"That may be so, but you mustn't talk about Pamyat here," he said. "It's a separate issue."

'The Pamyat people laughed and jeered, and when the sentence was read out some of them clapped and others said I'd got off too lightly. When some journalists asked them afterwards if the affair had done them any harm, they said: "His trial shows that the Zionists will be punished, and justice will triumph." And they said the same fate awaited all who tried to stop them . . .'

Some people would argue that in fact he had done them a huge favour, and others have even hinted that he might be in their pay . . .

'They cooked my goose at the trial for political reasons, of course. But I wasn't trying to change the world. I remember when I was young I read about a man living under German occupation who went up to a German officer in the street and shot him at point-blank range. And at Gestapo headquarters they told him: "Don't you realise you've not only killed the officer and yourself, but twenty more people who'll be shot in retaliation?" And the man replied: "I didn't want to change the course of the war, just to pay you back for killing my mother."

'I did what I did for all the silent people who thought words wouldn't change anything, or who wrote: "Dear Editor, We Soviet citizens wish to express our outrage . . ."

'For me there used to be neither Russians nor Jews. Now all that's in the past, and when I go out in the street it's as though everyone's staring at me. What is to become of my mother and me . . . ?'

Nationalism is a traditional outlet for social discontent, and anti-Semitism is the traditional lightning conductor for this discontent. We still refuse to take seriously the threat which Pamyat represents. Maybe journalists should take some of the blame for this: I used to avoid writing about 'nationalism', for fear of helping to fan the flames. Meanwhile the authorities sit back, and those who understand what's going on do nothing to stop it.

Consider the official warning from the Leningrad procurator, D. M. Veryovkin, to the leaders of the National Patriotic Pamyat Front, as they now call themselves, which recommended them to make a 'more objective assessment of historical and national events, and to ensure that their propaganda on the development of Russian national culture is based on a Marxist-Leninist position'. It can surely be no coincidence that these remarks were issued the day before Norinsky's trial.

Then Leningrad television, which is often quite good, made an exceptionally feeble programme about the Norinsky case in which a writer, a sociologist, and a teacher all failed to say anything of any significance about nationalism. Another coincidence? Just another infuriating case of Soviet unprofessionalism?

Various facts come together to suggest a tacit official sympathy for these criminals. Not one prosecutor has been named responsible for tracking them down, so that when the Moscow Fathers of Pamyat distribute leaflets calling for the 'Jewish usurpers and their guard-dogs' to be killed, they get away with it scot-free.

On leaving, Norinsky gave me several leaflets issued by Leningrad Pamyat. I already knew what to expect. Their 'Appeal to Russian

Students' to boycott Jewish teachers. Their 'Appeal to our Fellow-Countrymen' containing a mangled quote from a Tyutchev poem. 'The Crisis of the Triune Russian Nation', demanding that mixed-race marriages be banned . . .

'I've kept quiet all my life,' said Norinsky. 'But I never stopped thinking. People like me can be dangerous when they refuse to keep quiet any more . . .'

Norinsky's case reminds me of the parable of Balaam's ass. People who have been silent for decades must shout before learning to speak clearly. And how can we learn to speak clearly? By learning democracy. Internationalism and democracy are our only defence against nationalism.

'Please Entrust to my Care . . .'
Oleg Petrenko

It was a delightful, magical occasion. Russia's first professional ballet school, the Vaganova Academy of Choreography, was celebrating its 250th anniversary on the stage of Leningrad's Kirov Theatre of Opera and Ballet.

The Vaganova school has made an enormous contribution to Soviet and world ballet. Its pupils and teachers were showered with prizes and medals, huge celebrations were held in Moscow and Leningrad, and practically every publication in the country paid tribute to the cradle which had reared Pavlova, Nijinsky, Ulanova, Fokin, Lopukhov, and Grigorovich.

Its history goes back to the autumn of 1737, when the court ballet-master, Lande, appealed to the Empress Anna: 'I beg you to entrust to my care twelve Russian children, six males and six females, to create ballets and theatrical dances both comic and serious. Within three years these pupils will compare with the best foreign dancers . . .'

'Entrust to my care . . .' What fine, noble sentiments! Unfortunately they prevented me from enjoying the anniversary celebrations, and I couldn't shout 'bravo' as the adults received their awards, prizes, and honours. Instead I remembered a small boy I met last winter, sheltering from a blizzard by a pie stall on Razezhaya Street. I don't remember how we got into conversation, but I shall never forget my surprise when I learned that he was on his way to school – to be sick.

'For whose benefit?' I asked, joking.

'For my own,' he replied seriously. 'I shall be ill all day till evening, then go back to the boarding-house, and if my temperature isn't down by then I'll return to the sanitorium.'

I am as used as any other Soviet citizen to the paradoxes of the most free and humane medical system in the world, but this was something else . . .

It was this conversation that led me for the first time into the famous 'forge of ballet cadres' on Zodchy Rosso Street. The little boys and girls who were my guides on this joyless journey revealed no state secrets: everyone with access to such matters knows about the dilapidated state of the building, and the administrators have lost count of their petitions to the highest authorities. The school's many foreign visitors are regularly soothed by the phrase 'structural repairs'. But it's too late for cosmetic patch-up jobs now.

What the children showed me in the corners where guests are not brought (for fear of 'confusing' them) defied words. The peeling walls, the damp patches, the collapsing ceilings, and the innumerable other signs of advanced neglect – here was the reverse side of the 'romance of ballet'.

'What's the health department doing about this?' I demanded angrily, tripping over a plump grey-whiskered rat in a dark corridor, which had probably been terrorising the children since Petipa's time.

'Getting to the root of the problem!' the officials at the Kuibyshev district branch of this department announced proudly, rummaging around for a document they had presented five years ago to the head of the Leningrad department, which can refer complaints straight to the capital.

Not a trace of this brave document could be found, although I was shown files and files of fatherly advice sent every year to the school's administrators, recommending them in Aesopian tones to change either the Leningrad weather or the heartless administration of the Ministry of Culture. At least that was my interpretation of its years of complaints against the Vaganova's structural and technical deterioration.

'Do you know, there are only two tiny showers for 500 pupils!' department officials told me confidentially as I left.

'Why don't you close it, then?' I asked.

'The showers?' the department doctors said in surprise.

'No, the school. Until everything has been repaired.'

I may have been too categorical. Despite all the 'objective problems', as we say, the Vaganovites soldier on.

'Don't worry, my friend,' I remember saying patriotically to a visiting American shocked by the conditions there. 'Our eagles can soar in all weathers.'

Of course, the truth is that the Vaganovites are little troupers. One girl I know, who lives on a new housing estate in the suburbs of Leningrad, gets up at six every morning to be at Zodchy Rosso Street by nine. Every day she has nine lessons, followed by exercises and performances. She doesn't get home until late, and it's usually midnight before she finishes her normal school work and can go to bed. Yet she still thinks she has a good life, with her parents there to take care of the rest of her life for her.

Life is much harder for the boarders. No one would willingly exchange home for a hostel, and this isn't one of the most comfortable ones – eight or nine people to a room and a wretched buffet which closes early, so if you return late from a show you have to make do with some tap-water or wait for breakfast. It's also inconveniently far from any public transport to the school, and most children prefer to walk, which involves crossing four busy main roads. All this would be hard enough for a healthy child after a day of exhausting exercises. But what about those who are sick?

I confess I charged into the school's medical room full of righteous anger. But I soon calmed down, for here were the kindest, cosiest people these children were likely to find. Every spare moment between classes they run in here to drink tea and chat, and the medical workers treat them like their own children, doing as much as they possibly can for them within the limits of their tiny staff and budget.

The pupils here have much more to do with medicine than most other children. Muscle strain and other injuries are an inevitable part of their profession, and their dusty, airless existence, and the insanely adult pressures they have to endure, do little for their health. Yet these years are rebuilding their entire organism, and laying the physiological basis of their future life.

I have watched our sports stars training, but the selfless discipline of these still unknown boys and girls is no less arduous. It's not yet a matter of an all-consuming love of art, but pride and a fierce spirit of competition are there the moment a child steps inside these gates at the age of ten or eleven. Out of hundreds of applicants for a place in the sun only seventy boys and girls are selected, and this selection is conditional, since five of their eight years of study are probationary. It's not enough to be gifted and a good student, they also have to work terribly hard, and at any moment their dreams may be shattered by injury, illness, weight-gain, or changes to the growing body.

The verdict is always final, without the right to appeal, and years of hard work may end in tragedy, with the child being sent back to its ordinary school.

I feel so sorry for the losers, and I am sure there would be far fewer of them if the conditions of their life and the very adult burdens they bear corresponded even minimally to our much-vaunted 'care of the younger generation'.

Alas, the only truly impressive piece of equipment I saw in the medical room was some magnificent Firbanks scales on castors. This gleaming nickel beauty is over a hundred years old, and knows to the last ounce the weight of our flowering Russian ballet.

The school's remaining equipment (apart from a recently acquired pressure chamber) is rather less than one would see in an average factory clinic. Where are the physiotherapy and massage rooms, the swimming-pool, and all the other basics one would expect to find at any sports training centre?

Presumably the pupils are at least given a specially planned diet, based on their extra expenditure of energy and vitamin requirements? In theory, yes: a scientific menu has been worked out for them by chefs from the Military Medical Academy. But getting hold of the actual foodstuffs is another matter. I have only just learnt that schools throughout our country (with the exception of the Baltic republics) are forbidden to give children fresh cottage-cheese which hasn't been heat-treated. The Vaganova would love to give the children some of this light, nourishing food for breakfast. And it's cheap too, which is a major advantage in the winter, when black caviare and green vegetables are out of the question.

A young sportsman representing his country abroad is allotted four roubles thirty-five kopecks a day for food alone, and an adult gets six, eight, even twelve roubles, depending on his rank. Meanwhile the *total* daily allowance for each child here is just one rouble seventy-two kopecks.

For them the competition continues all the year round, and the sacrifices are as great as those of any champion. Only for them it's not medals that are at stake, but their entire future. Even so I was disturbed to see sick pupils having to join in the exercises.

'What can we do?' say the doctors sadly. 'There's no nurse to look after them at the boarding-house, and we have no one here to stay with them at night. So they have to travel back and forth.'

The sick ones often sleep in the communal dormitories, exposing the others to the risk of infection. If they're very ill they'll be sent to hospital, of course. But that's just a last resort. So the children prefer to put up with a high temperature, and if illness strikes during the exam season they'll go to classes straight from the sanitorium.

'Why are you so stoical?' I naïvely asked one of the boys. 'Surely you can take your exams later?'

'It's a matter of timing,' he explained. 'I work and train all year so as to be in top form for these exams. If I miss them I'll lose my momentum and burn myself out.'

Timing is certainly something the school can boast of. What is catastrophically lacking is any proper attention from the Ministry of Culture, whose attitude to this unique 'cradle of the Russian ballet' reminds one of our former Ministry of Education's relationship with some benighted village school.

The latest budget has been drawn up partly on the basis of reports issued twenty-seven years ago, when there were 400 pupils. There are already 504, however, and the rouble is worth quite a bit less now than it was then. I was told that the school received a grant, but what kind of grant can this be when parents have to pay 56 roubles a month for their children's board, the children themselves earn 10,000 roubles a year from performances, and there still isn't enough to go round?

The director, L. Nadirov, along with A. Meshcherin and his colleagues at the medical centre, must be given all credit for their heroic commitment and hard work. According to Meshcherin, money for medical supplies suddenly became available on the eve of the anniversary celebrations, which meant they could order some badly needed apparatus and buy the children vitamins. But their hopes are all pinned on the structural repairs and restoration which have finally been promised for the years 1990 to 1993.

The Ministry's next official reply will doubtless refer to this, along with a detailed account of the blessings which will fall on the Vaganovites' heads – before, we hope, the ceilings do. The executive committee of the Leningrad Soviet has even named the organisations which will undertake the work, and the committee's vice-president has been made personally responsible for it.

So why do I feel so sad about the past?

Because I can at least see it with my own eyes, whereas I don't have much faith in the 'bright future'. I remember all too well the magnificent promises surrounding such cultural projects as the

Leningrad Public Library, where repairs dragged on for so many years. And now we see a whole generation of boys and girls facing a very uncertain childhood.

This is why I wasn't over-delighted with the splendid celebrations, or with all the medals presented on the stage of the Kirov Theatre. Alas, it has proved far easier to mark the school's anniversary than to repair it. And to celebrate it at the expense of children who live on the cold porridge cooked for them by uncaring adults.

The Week of Conscience
Olga Nemirovskaya

A building in Moscow's Zhuravlev Square in which Lenin used to speak was rebuilt after the war as the Palace of Culture of the Moscow Electric Lightbulb Factory, where Stalin elected himself to supreme power. In November 1988 this was the venue for a 'Week of Conscience', of which Ogonyok *was a leading sponsor. The wheel thus turns full circle. The building once identified with* his *power and* his *despotism is now a memorial to* his *victims.*

We had worried that people wouldn't respond. But they braved howling winds and slushy snow, and by the middle of the first day thousands of them were queuing at the door and crowding into the palace's vast foyer and club-rooms.

They waited patiently. We had all waited so long for this moment when it would be possible to lay flowers at some symbolic grave, to

Queue for the Week of Conscience

remember our own family and others, and to play our part in the reconstruction of truth and justice.

Many people bring flowers. They place them on a camp barrow in front of a brick wall depicting a map of the Gulag. Kolyma, Akmolinsk, Taishet, Norilsk, Vorkuta, Igarka. The dents on the brickwork are like bullet marks. Special-regime camps, where prisoners were subjected to refined tortures before being shot. Political isolation camps, 'Mountain camps', 'Steppe camps' . . .

People put their flowers on the barrow, as well as donations for the Memorial Fund (six and a half thousand roubles in the first day alone), then stand gazing at the sinister dents on the map. What do they see? The suffering of their loved ones? Lives destroyed? Liberty shattered? Honour and dignity crushed? Everyone here has their own spot on the map. Yet not everyone has relatives who died. There are many young people too, for whom it's desperately important to learn what happened.

People stand by the white canvas surface of the Wall of Memory. Pinned to it are photographs and documents about the rehabilitations, newspaper cuttings from the sixties and eighties and brief biographical notes. 'Ivan Mikhailovich Martemyanov, a poor peasant with nine children, from the village of Blagoveshchensk. Arrested 1937. Fate unknown. Rehabilitated 1960.' And there is a photograph of Martemyanov with his family.

A row of six photographs are accompanied by a note from K. A.

Dudinskaya, from the town of Gorky. 'None of my family came back.' And her words are like a cry of pain.

Many entire families were destroyed. The Kiryanens lost thirteen people, and the Pyustonens, from a village near Leningrad, lost ten.

Happy, handsome young couples gaze out at us. One day he is denounced as an 'enemy of the people', and she becomes the wife of a 'traitor to the motherland'. A short note informs us that Vasily Basyubin, manager of the country's main hydroelectric plant, was arrested in 1937 and died in a camp, that his wife, a surgeon, was arrested along with him, and that their daughter, Svetlana, was born and brought up in the camp.

It's the photographs that strike one first on the Wall of Memory. What handsome, intelligent faces! Yes, only the best were chosen to be destroyed.

The mound of flowers keeps growing and people keep arriving, yet everyone is very quiet. I can't be the only one here with a lump in my throat. It isn't easy to relive such a terrible past.

People crowd together, reading, thinking, looking. A woman sits down and scribbles on a piece of paper 'Please will anyone who met Atom Sharikyan in Karaganda camp contact me,' and she pins it to the board with her name and address.

There are many such notes. Another, pinned to the side of the wall, says: 'Grigory Naimovich Khotimsky, president of the State Planning Department of the Ukraine. Arrested 1935 in Kiev. Not heard of since. His wife and two sons also died.'

The information centre in the hall is overflowing with people bearing documents and information about those killed. Wives, children, grandchildren, relatives, and friends stand in silent lines in front of the desks. No tears, no hysterics. Life has taught them not to cry, however much they long to do so. Here from Orekhovo-Zuevo is the son of Konstantin Levkoev, a lawyer at an oxygen-cylinder plant, who was arrested in 1941 and died in jail in 1942. Both his sons fought at the front throughout the war and survived. I wondered if they had fought at Stalingrad . . .

Nina Kanysheva's father, Konstantin Banin, a party member since 1918 and a member of the Kursk regional executive, was arrested and shot. Nina Kanysheva says she is campaigning for the establishment of a small memorial to the atrocities in Kursk.

Lina Dubinina married a member of the German anti-fascist Left Column theatre group, who came to live in the Soviet Union in 1932.

Here they appeared in a popular film called *Fighters*, about the burning of the Reichstag, in which Lina Dubinina's husband, Bruno Schmitdorf, played the leading role. In 1937 Lina Dubinina was arrested and ordered to denounce her husband and his German friends as spies. She refused, and was exiled to Orenburg; shortly afterwards all the members of the Left Column were jailed, and all copies of the film destroyed except one, which later turned up in the GDR.

The stands in the Information Centre contain lists of 27,000 names. Dmitry Yurasov, a student at Moscow's Institute of Historical Archives, has been keeping card-index records of Stalin's victims since he was fourteen, 'because this was all that interested me'. For the Week of Conscience Yurasov has compiled information from the military collegium of the Supreme Court about 15,000 people rehabilitated in 1955.

People from numerous industries and commissariats were killed, and Yurasov has drawn up a list of those who disappeared from the commissariats of heavy industry and communications. Beside this he has set some of his card-index data about leading members of the Union of Writers, and the names of those who have been posthumously rehabilitated. He lists the casualties at just one university, Sverdlovsk, where twelve teachers and scientists were killed. And he gives one brief, revealing statistic: of 186 members and candidate members of the Party Central Committee between the VIIth and XVIIth congresses, 111 were shot.

The next stand displays information which has probably never been shown before. These are the names of Cheka agents, NKVD generals, and regional bosses who were in charge of the arrests and set up the local 'troikas'. Here we see endless lists of NKVD agents, who in 1937 received the Order of Lenin, the Red Star, and the Red Banner 'for exemplary services to the struggle against the workers' enemies', or 'for selfless services to the state'. These are the people who tormented, tortured, and destroyed their victims. Against some of their names is the word 'shot', although presumably many more of them are still walking around with their medals today.

Dmitry Yurasov says: 'All of this work is still "unofficial", although it may push the government into opening up the archives. A year ago I wouldn't have dreamt we could gather so much information from all over the country. Of course, my information is far from complete; I just use it as a sort of sociological cross-section. But I can tell you that the people who suffered most were the ordinary workers, peasants, and officials, whose names never appear in our history books. We're talking here about millions of real, living people, each of them with a name. We must never forget this, or we'll end up like Stalin: here's a person and there's a problem; no more person, no more problem.'

All this work is unfolding against the background of the photographic records of the 1930s and 1940s. What trust and enthusiasm there was then, what strong, happy people with their open, cheerful faces, who seemed to fill the air with their enthusiasm.

Looming over the celebrations and demonstrations of 1935 were banners and slogans proclaiming: 'Stalin is Our Guiding Light', and 'We Love Comrade Stalin, Best Friend of Athletes'. A banner from a photograph of the building of the Magnitogorsk hydroelectric station in 1929 exhorts: 'Let Us Open New Workshops Armed with the Six Historic Commands of Comrade Stalin.' And so on, and so on . . .

How did people put up with it? The answer is that they were sent to prison and shot before they had the chance to entertain any doubts; we toiled and dreamed and believed then, and to betray that optimism was seen as a heinous crime.

There has been much talk at memorial meetings throughout this week of the price we paid for our excessive idealism, and speakers have emphasised again and again how important it is to learn to see through the myths to the reality.

'In 1945 I was only nineteen, but I can still remember being keenly aware of the dishonesty around me,' says Yury Sergeevich Tsizin, now a respected chemist. In 1945, Tsizin and his student friends were arrested, charged under Article 58/10 of the Criminal Code★ and packed off to a camp. 'I was a lot luckier than my friends,' he says. 'The youngest of us, who was only sixteen and a talented mathematician, got the longest sentence and the heaviest workload, and he was never able to use his mathematics.'

Again and again people return to this theme of unfulfilled talents and wasted possibilities. Entire systems of thought, literary movements, and scientific and artistic schools were demolished. The unique and the brilliant were wiped off the face of the earth and their memory obliterated. The Soviet republics had their indigenous

★ See 'Matryona's Crime', p. 209.

intelligentsia destroyed and the continuity of their national traditions extinguished. 'How vile to shoot a star,' wrote Yunna Moritz of the Georgian poet Galaktion Tabidze. But her words could apply to any artist.

It's not only we who mourn this break in continuity. A few days before the Week of Conscience, British actors in London organised an evening dedicated to the memory of Stalin's victims, at which they collected money for the Memorial.

We need historical truth above all else, but we shall only restore it bit by bit. The true extent of the losses during the siege of Leningrad is at last coming out, for instance, revealing figures which were the subject of such an official storm that even in the seventies they were twice removed from Marshal Zhukov's books on the subject.

Yet throughout the week, one speaker after another warned that there are no sudden changes in history, and that although the Stalin era is now over, Stalin is still with us.

Everyone was invited to take part in the preliminary exhibition of plans for the Memorial.

'We don't want a pompous monument,' said some people from Leningrad, to whom the Memorial will be dedicated. 'We want an educational and research centre for studying the Stalin period as it relates to the entire history of our state.'

'I'd like to see a simple monument depicting a group of people which should include a teenager,' said others, 'because Stalin's laws allowed children to be tortured and imprisoned. There should also be a length of railway track, because life in the camps centred on the railways.'

People continue to pour into Zhuravlev Square. The Week of Conscience has turned the Palace of Culture of the Moscow Electric Lightbulb Factory into a prototype of the future Memorial . . .

Arctic Silence?
Yury Rytkheu

There have been a number of suggestions recently that the indigenous tribes of the Soviet Arctic should be housed in reservations.

Apart from a few showcase Indian reservations in the USA, most reservations there are regarded as a national disgrace – filthy places ruled by poverty, ignorance, and alcoholism. Rumours of reservations rich in oil and precious minerals are mere fairy-tales for the uneducated. Yet the idea is only the logical result of Russia's traditional attitude to the people of the Far North.

Russia's colonisation of the polar regions started in the early seventeenth century. The newcomers regarded the fur-clad savages they met there as an inferior species, and these first encounters tended to end in bloodshed. But native resistance was fierce too, and a senate decree of 1742 gave orders to 'advance on the turbulent Chukchi with armed might, and extirpate them'.

Many ethnic northerners, isolated by vast distances and impenetrable forests, continued for centuries with a way of life that had been established before the Egyptian Pharaohs. Yet those who came into contact with the 'white man' degenerated rapidly, and by the early twentieth century the number of settlements on the shores of the Chukchi peninsula had been reduced by more than two-thirds.

In the first years of Soviet power, the party's first emissaries to the Far North won the local people's hearts with their sincerity and enthusiasm, and new schools and cultural centres were built.

Yet as oil workers, miners, and other settlers poured into the region, more and more villages were wiped out. This process involved the wholesale destruction of unique Arctic tribes such as the Naukay Eskimos, who were transferred bodily to the Chukot village of Nunyamo then dispersed amongst various other hamlets, thus obliterating a living bridge between the ancient cultures of the Eastern and Western hemispheres, the Old and the New Worlds.

Natural resources were recklessly exploited to make way for mines, quarries, and oil wells. Native people were robbed of their reindeer pastures and hunting areas. The fish and wildlife which formed the basis of their way of life were destroyed. Spawning rivers and walrus breeding-grounds were polluted, and local traditions were steadily eroded to accommodate the influx of foreign settlers.

Collective farms were converted into state farms, promising people a monthly salary. Real money twice a month to buy drink proved a great inducement, and the newly created 'workers' soon realised that they could get paid for doing no work at all.

By the late 1950s, the publication of ethnic-language literature and textbooks was being restricted, and the teacher at our village school burnt all Eskimo textbooks as 'holding up children's development towards a bright future'. By the 1960s, the ethnic languages were no longer being taught in the schools, so that most students at the national teacher-training college at Anadyr no longer even know their own language.

The problems of the North were handled until recently by distant officials in the Soviet of Ministers' Department of Northern Affairs, who had very little idea where the North actually was. Many of these time-servers were friends of the first secretary of the Ryazan provincial party committee, who strutted around with his medals before being exposed for his part in an infamous local government fraud.

Throughout the years of personality cult, muddled experiments, drunkenness, and stagnation, many admirable initiatives were reduced to mere slogans. Government and scientific bodies organised conferences, symposiums, and seminars, and published decrees, instructions, and resolutions, most of which remained on paper, or were used by the bureaucratic apparatus to its own advantage.

The statistics for these years of 'unprecedented prosperity' are grim indeed. Reindeer herds declined and marine trapping petered out. Northerners' health, formerly the envy of the country, was undermined by alcoholism and innumerable infections. To this day the number of TB clinics is not declining. Nor are the 'special schools' for alcoholics' children who have been born physically and mentally handicapped. And even official statistics now admit that hundreds of native families have nowhere to live.

As personal responsibility was steadily eroded, our splendid education system became a way of removing parents' responsibilities for their children; I remember once staying with an old friend who apologised that his children were 'under our feet' while their boarding-school was being decorated.

In the 1920s the polar explorers Nansen and Amundsen insisted that the only chance of saving the northern people was to isolate them from all contact with civilisation. The idea was not seriously considered at the time, but it seems relatively benign in the face of recent plans to 'integrate' the indigenous people into the world of the settlers, thereby obliterating their native traditions, languages, occupations, and cultural identity. This has happened already to the entire Chukot–Eskimo population of Nunyamo, who were transferred to the district capital of Lavrentiya, where former nomads, whalers, and fishermen are now loaders, stokers, and cleaners for the settlers who run the town.

I once visited the ancient Chukot hamlet of Enmylin, where the local boarding-school, the nursery-school, the post office, the dispensary, boilerhouse, and farm were all run by Russians. Most of these people, however much they claimed to love the local population, were only there because of the money. I spoke to the boiler-man, who told me that he had a university degree, but was paid far more here than someone with a doctorate would be in his home town on the Volga.

Yet even in hard times, there have always been people who refused to keep silent. People such as Dr Alexander Wolfson and Vladilen Leontev, whose lives are shining examples of a properly civilised relationship with the 'national minorities'.

I first met Alexander Wolfson over thirty years ago in the Chukot settlement of Lorino, where he was the district doctor. Even the most remote nomadic reindeer herdsman had heard of Wolfson. He collected some fascinating health statistics on the Chukot people, tracing a clear connection between Chukotka's death and suicide rate and its worsening social climate, its increasing alcoholism, and its inadequate housing provisions. These gruesome figures were hastily hushed up, and medical 'politicians' quickly manufactured new ones in their place.

Vladilen Leontev was an ethnographer and writer. The son of a partisan from the Far East, he had come to our village with his parents in the late thirties, and had sat next to me at school. We grew up together: he taught us Russian and we taught him Chukot, and after graduating from university he returned to Uelen, where he became director of our village school. As fluent in our language as he was in Russian, he translated several books into Chukot, wrote many scholarly works of research on ethnic linguistics and ethnography, and was the author of a number of literary works on the people who became his own.

These two men, one Russian, the other Jewish, were both branded 'Chukot nationalists', and local KGB agents started checking up on them.

Now at last the true state of affairs, previously veiled by a coy cloud of propaganda, is being revealed, and people in the land of the traditional Arctic silence are starting to speak up for themselves.

I am against reservations. Living on a reservation curtails people's civil rights, and excludes them from any participation in social affairs. This is why Hitler's plans for a conquered Russia involved herding the Russian people into reservations and exterminating them there.

Small nations have the same rights as any other in the Soviet Union, and want to help build a genuine socialism which will give an equal chance to every race and individual, regardless of their origins.

Unwanted?
E. Skvortsova

6 February 1988. A seven-day-old baby is found on the staircase of the soldiers' waiting-room at Moscow's Byelorussian Station.

30 April 1988. A woman carrying a six-month-old baby knocks at the door of a flat and informs its occupants that she is a friend of their son, whom they are anxious to trace. The woman puts the baby on the sofa and leaves. The occupants wait for her for forty minutes, then phone the police.

2 July 1988. At 6 p.m. on the platform of the Izmailovsky underground station, nineteen-year-old Tatyana Sherekina is approached by an unknown woman who hands her a new-born baby and asks her to hold it for a few moments while she goes to the lavatory. The woman does not return.

These babies usually go straight from the police to the Sixth Children's Home, at 40 Pyatnitskaya Street. 'Most of them are of unknown parentage,' says Galina Pichkova, chief doctor at the home. 'A woman can always leave her unwanted baby at the hospital. But she'll be under a lot of pressure not to, and rather than have to fill in a lot of forms many of them just discharge themselves and dump the baby in the street.

'The number of babies varies enormously depending on the time of year. Most of them are conceived during the summer holidays. That means they're born in the spring, and come to us around April.'

These babies' problems start from the first moments of their life. Since doctors know next to nothing about where they come from or whether they suffer from any congenital disorders, they're not usually put up for adoption. Instead they face a life of communal canteens and dormitories, shared toys, medicines, and friends in misfortune, and a trail of official paperwork which will follow them around for virtually the rest of their lives.

However impressive the Sixth Children's Home may be, no institution can adequately care for a child's needs. This is why so many countries employ professional foster-mothers to look after such children. It must be possible to organise some such thing here.

Nor does their ordeal end when they leave care. Most face life outside with no roof over their head. Those whose mothers are in prison are relatively fortunate, for they will still be legally registered in her former home. A few may have the good luck to get a bed in their workplace hostel. But most of these hostels are only for people from out of town, and the child's birth certificate will give its place of birth as Moscow.

Despite the critical shortages which plague our country, it must be possible for institutions like the Children's Fund to ensure that a certain number of flats are allocated to these children every year. Surrounded by indifference, without any public acknowledgement of their plight, our spring foundlings deserve at least these basic requirements of life.

'You Don't Scare Me, Psychiatrist!'
Nina Chugunova
and Vladimir Voevoda

The Greeks threw stones at the mad. The fascists exterminated them. The Russians regarded them as holy, took them into the monasteries, and built sanctuaries for them. Moscow's Pokrov Cathedral, built by Barma and Postnik to commemorate the victory over Kazan and Astrakhan, is better known as the Cathedral of Vasily the Blessed, one of the most famous of the capital's holy fools.

Ignorance and fear predispose people to mysticism, predestination, and prophecy, or to take the most monstrous reprisals against such things. (Remember Tendryakov's terrible story about the mad prophetess in the 1930s, who paralysed an entire region with terror.) Ignorance and fear also produced the Lysenko school of psychiatry, with its now notorious delusions about the ability of one phenomenon to change into another, such as a neurosis into a pathological disorder.

Scientific backwardness bore macabre results for those who became helpless victims of political intrigue, and doctors acquired unprecedented power over people. For years psychiatry was totally isolated from society by the impenetrable walls of the mental institutions and our own distrust. People who were mentally ill were literally incarcerated within these walls, and might be subjected to treatment which was more reminiscent of punishment. Mental illness because something shameful, frightening, and dangerous, and to be suspected of it even more so. These are the origins of our present-day attitudes to mental illness.

According to the experts, neuroses are behavioural disorders induced by negative conditions. If this is so, we should be seeing neuroses on a massive scale in our society. Yet the fear of mental illness makes it almost impossible for doctors to treat the preliminary symptoms of a disorder. This explains why the splendid psychiatric unit in one Moscow hospital is only half full, while the suicide rate amongst those with serious mental conditions is on the increase.

The main reason our doctors don't catch mental illness in time, however, is our 'registration' system. 'Registration' is a terrible word. Someone driven to seek treatment to avoid a nervous break-down may go to the doctor complaining of insomnia or irritability, and come out a 'registered' mental patient, their future in ruins.

The Presidium of the Supreme Soviet last year issued new instructions on psychiatric treatment, which ordered an end to the registration system. But discrimination against mental patients is still widespread. We are now beginning to discover how many quite 'normal' young men doing their military service are simply not up to all the various army drills and 'traditions'. Yet a young man who commits some minor misdemeanour is still defenceless against a tyrannical army doctor who chooses to put a virtually ineradicable mark on his army card denoting mental illness.

Those in charge of the offices and factories employing such patients usually wash their hands of them rather than try to help them. Meanwhile someone having a nervous breakdown may still get a sick-note with the dreaded 'registration' on it, and will then have to face endless victimisation from society at large.

All this explains why people prefer to stagger on blindly without help or support until they reach breaking-point, and so another person is lost to society.

Special Region
Anatoly Golovkov

*Ogonyok special investigator Golovkov has just returned
from a visit to the Transcaucasus, where he stayed in Georgia
and the Nagorno-Karabakh Autonomous Region of
Azerbaijan. This is the first of two reports, from the NKAR.*

Blessed are the merciful: for they shall obtain mercy.

Matthew 5:7

When we allow people a taste of mercy, they rejoice in it.

Koran, Sura 30, Rumy 35

Stepanakert, Spring 1989

Anyone visiting this town for the first time will find a lot that is new
and a lot to get used to. We must get used to the fact that this isn't just
another region of the Soviet Union, but a special territory, governed
by its own special rules; that power resides not with the regional
executive committee or the local party, but with the Special Administrative Committee of the Nagorno-Karabakh Autonomous Region;
that you need a passport or special military pass to enter the area; that
if you're told to stop your car you'd better slam on the brakes and not
ask questions; that there is a curfew between the hours of 1 and
5 a.m.; that tough men in army fatigues, bullet-proof vests, and
helmets are now the harsh reality of the Special Region.

It is all quiet in Stepanakert now. There are no demonstrations, no
meetings, and on the surface it seems as though there's nothing
wrong. As though a certain Kevorkov, whose very glance used to
shrivel up everything for miles around, had not been marched one
night, pale and trembling, to Stepanakert's party offices, surrounded
by police, where crowds ordered the boss of the region to stop lying
to Moscow about 'a handful of extremists stirring up trouble', and to

send the Party Central Committee a telegram explaining the true state of affairs . . .

It is all quiet in Stepanakert. The lights are on in the offices of the Special Committee until long after midnight. From time to time gangs of people throw stones at buses and smash their windows, or daub obscene messages on the carriages of trains. But this is as nothing compared to the events of last year. And in the fields around the village of Kuropatkino, where many collective farms have already prepared their arable land for sowing, there isn't a fence in sight, and Armenians and Azerbaijanis work side by side.

Someone visiting Nagorno-Karabakh for the first time will sooner or later have to ask themself some hard questions. But it's not easy to get to the truth through the web of accumulated emotions and the few brief lines in the newspapers. Even Lenin, on his pedestal outside the regional party offices, is silent.

A chain reaction of reciprocal claims, provocations, and clashes has developed into an uncontrolled mass psychosis. An ethnic political conflict has burst into the open and managed to involve some eleven and a half million people. A peaceful movement of Karabakhi Armenians, whose demands the authorities either would not or dared not consider in time, has resulted in the blood, pain, and suffering of countless innocent people, both Azerbaijanis and Armenians . . .

We already know how Yerevan and Baku responded to the Karabakh movement. While I was in Moscow I spoke on the telephone to the Baku ethnographer Eduard Namizov.

'Early in December 1988, several thousand people held a meeting here,' he told me. 'A number of historians, sociologists, and ethnographers warned the authorities that the mood in the square was very tense, and that they should stay out of it and wait for things to simmer down. But they took no notice, and dispersed the meeting with great violence. What did they achieve? It was virtually impossible for them to control the thugs who then rampaged through the town, and there were several outbreaks of violence. Before the meeting was dispersed, these criminals had been attacking everyone they came across. Now they suddenly turned into "patriots" and set upon the Armenians. Two years before, the same thing happened in Sumgait. Some professors there too had warned the authorities that the situation was fraught with violence. But there too they didn't listen, and sure enough violence erupted . . .'

Our political consciousness has reached a new phase. Everyone is suddenly fixated on the sovereignty of the republics. But what does this sovereignty mean? Economically and culturally it means virtually nothing. There merely remains the sovereignty of borders. But revising borders would mean the start of an endless process of transferring territories from one authority to another, and we'd end by carving up the entire map of the Soviet Union, with local authorities having artificially to maintain the ethnic equilibrium.

The real nub of Karabakh's problems is some 300,000 homeless Armenian and Azerbaijani refugees, crippled and exhausted by misery and anger, living in terrible poverty. These people were the first disillusioning blow to the new politics which started stirring in our country in the spring of 1985.

Nationalism can warp a person's mind and turn them into a mutant. It can also revive lost national pride, honour, and solidarity. That is why the people of Karabakh sometimes appear to be betrayed by their memory, and to forget that Armenians, Azerbaijanis, Russians, Jews, and everyone else in the area were equally oppressed by Kevorkov and his cronies. That Azerbaijanis stood shoulder to shoulder with Armenians at the first spring meetings last year. Not because they agreed with all their demands, but because they'd stood together like this for decades.

Now, however, they will never forget the cowardice of the local party leadership. Or the lies the authorities told to Baku and Moscow, knowing full well that they were playing with fire. Now, say what you like about everyone on earth being brothers – that there are no bad nations, only individual deviants and weak leaders – people will always remember Askeran, Sumgait, and the houses burnt last September in Shusha and Stepanakert.

All this will be remembered . . .

THE TRUTH WE NEED

I met dozens of people, both Armenian and Azerbaijani, during my stay in Nagorno-Karabakh, and before I left Moscow I read all the newspapers and watched all the television broadcasts. I therefore considered myself quite well prepared for my meeting with these people, especially since some journalist friends had returned last year from Nagorno-Karabakh and had talked for hours, sometimes with tears in their eyes, about everything they'd seen and heard.

They then wrote it all up. But practically no one would publish it.

Someone at the top had taken a decision, not only for the journalists but for their chief editors and their millions of readers too, as to whether society needed the truth or not, and if so what sort of truth.

Articles by Nikolai Andreev, *Ogonyok*'s Vladimir Chernov, and several other journalists all sank without trace, unprinted and rejected by their editors. True, one could always hear the honest voice of *Izvestiya*'s Pavel Gutionov, and if one was lucky one could get hold of a copy of *Aurora*, containing a fine piece by Alexander Vasilevsky. But everyone understood that honest articles would warm people's hearts there, and dishonest ones would provoke strikes.

In my desperate search for some alternative before I left for Nagorno-Karabakh, I remembered my friends in Baku and Yerevan. I thought of Gaika Kotandzhian, who openly criticised the Yerevan party bureaucrat Demirchyan. Of the artist and modeller Raf Sardarov, an internationalist by spirit and conviction. And of the writer Akram Ailisli, whom I do not know, but who gave an interview to the Baku newspaper *Watchtower* on 12 March of this year.

Ailisli said: 'Some people are prepared to shout their heads off to the crowds, who want nothing more than to bask in the words of these spiritual swindlers whom they embrace as their "chosen ones" and "fathers of the people" . . .'

And: 'We won't achieve progress, on the national question or any other, with a lot of ignorant, irresponsible demands and slogans. Progress is the fruit of reason.'

Akram Ailisli didn't wait to speak out. The memory was evidently still fresh in his mind of the thousands of people who rampaged through Baku last winter, waving green flags and demanding punishment for subversives. And yet the Russian intelligentsia, from whom Yerevan, Baku, and Stepanakert were so eagerly awaiting some word, had practically nothing to say about the intercommunal conflict.

Even *Ogonyok* said nothing, knowing that elements of the bureaucracy would be quick to accuse us of playing up to one side or another. Silence last year became a political position. Stalin died thirty-six years ago, but there are still plenty of his admirers around. Just show them the next 'enemy of the people', drop a few hints, and hey presto, the machine will go smoothly into action.

Chronicle of Events

18 September 1988 At 6.30 p.m., a meeting authorised by the local authorities takes place on Stepanakert's Victory Square. An hour later, news reaches the meeting of clashes in the village of Khodzhalla. Some leave the meeting for Khodzhalla, and at about nine that evening fighting breaks out between inhabitants of the town and the village, in which people on both sides are wounded. On the same evening, Armenians and Azerbaijanis in Shusha and Stepanakert start setting fire to each other's houses, and there are fights and massacres.

21 September A curfew and state of emergency is announced in the territory of the NKAR and the Agdam region of Azerbaijan.

SPLIT

Blood flowed in Nagorno-Karabakh. But most people, still apparently deluded by the latest official information, continued to blame 'extremists'. Of course it's always much easier to implant an idea in people's minds than to dispel it, especially if this involves admitting mistakes. Maybe it has become clearer with hindsight that the conflict in the Caucasus has nothing to do with 'anti-Soviet plots'. That one might disagree about the meetings in Baku, for instance, but one must take the views of the Azerbaijanis into account; and that despite the huge unpopularity of the Krunk, it was really nothing more than fifty people, elected by open ballot.* Krunk is finished now anyway, disbanded on orders from above. But the fact is that a large number of former Krunk members are now working to promote stability in the region. One of them is president of the town's executive committee, and others are local factory directors or members of the intelligentsia.

After a year of uninterrupted meetings and strikes in Karabakh, one could understand how 'corrupt elements' might have the power to run certain branches of trade and industry, but not to bring 100,000 people on to the streets of Baku and Yerevan.

The tragedy of the Karabakh movement is that no one had the courage to send a proper political assessment of the situation to Sumgait. For this, the relatives of those killed in Karabakh, Yerevan, and even Baku should give special thanks to Kyamran Mamedogly

---

*Krunk (the name means 'Flying Crane' in Armenian) was an informal nationalist-inspired association in Nagorno-Karabakh with the avowed purpose of 'politically activating the workers and intelligentsia'.

Bagirov, who rushed back and forth like a madman between Stepanakert, Moscow, and Baku. Thanks are due also to his wise teacher, Geidar Alievich Aliev. It was these men who did all they possibly could to show the rest of the Soviet Union that the Sumgait massacres were merely a case of 'hooliganism'.

Wise and farseeing was Geidar Aliev, First Secretary of the Central Committee of the Communist Party of Azerbaijan! After Aliev told his people that the party leadership of the republic wasn't against Islam, the Muslim religion rapidly gained strength and support in Azerbaijan. ('At work I'm a Communist,' one party official told me seven years ago. 'At home though, sorry, I'm a Muslim!') The spread of Islam was paralleled by a surge of popular nationalism. Of course it would be foolish to see Azerbaijani chauvinism as something 'inherent', as some Armenians are prone to do. But we have to make some sense of this present craze for nationalism – be it Yerevan's Muslim Dashnaks, the extreme right-wing Mussavitists, or our own home-grown Russian Pamyat group.

There are virtually no Azerbaijanis left now in the seventy districts of Armenia. There isn't one Armenian in the Nagorno-Karabakh town of Shusha, in Agdam, or in any of the traditional Azerbaijani villages. There are hardly any Armenians in Azerbaijan, and if any have returned it's certainly not the 40,000 that *Komsomolskaya Pravda* told its readers about on 15 March this year. The split has gone very deep. Three hundred thousand refugees are sadistically herded from place to place. It's impossible to keep a tally of the reciprocal insults. The madness has surely reached its limit.

Why have the Armenians fled from so many other places besides Sumgait? Because they were more or less pushed out, as were the Azerbaijanis living in Armenia. You don't have much choice when your local state farm director or party secretary says straight out: 'Sorry, comrade, but I can no longer guarantee your safety. Better pack your bags and move.'

It must now be said loud and clear that both Azerbaijanis and Armenians behaved with inexcusable savagery in driving people from their 'second homelands'. And of course the authorities in Armenia could no more answer for the bearded young men in black shirts than those in Azerbaijan could for the 'activists' in red headbands. It's a strange kind of segregation that we socialists are witnessing, in which people who have built homes and brought in the harvest together for decades suddenly wake up one day as enemies.

Chronicle of Events

12 January 1989 The Supreme Soviet announces the 'Special Administration of the NKAR'.

5 March From an interview in *Soviet Karabakh* with the President of the NKAR Special Administrative Committee, Arkady Ivanovich Volsky:

Q. 'Many say that after the state of emergency, soldiers disarmed only Armenians.'

A. 'From last September, 3,502 weapons were removed or confiscated outright. 1,923 of these were from Armenians, 1,579 from Azerbaijanis.'

At least these confiscated guns won't be the cause of any more deaths. The Committee has been busy imposing order, without the use of force, since 20 January, when it assumed power. Apart from a few cases of petty hooliganism, not one person has been detained or arrested. The armoured personnel-carriers decorating the streets since last autumn have driven off, and the number of patrols have been reduced. But the tension is still there. You can't see it, but you can feel it. Little groups of people stand whispering at the crossroads under the gaze of internal security troops and police. Foolish rumours occasionally flit through the town. Unrepeatably obscene leaflets continually land on the committee members' desks.

6–12 March Strike in Stepanakert. Cause: rumours, lies and leaflets, distributed by some evil hand.

This strike was totally unexpected; it surprised not only the members of the Committee but the former Krunk members too.

It seems strange that despite the suspension of the local organs of Soviet power, the Committee's new emergency powers, and the fact that no one in the Special Region dared do anything without its approval, it nonetheless had difficulty maintaining order in the region.

Factory directors who only last December had been in virtual control, and were now completely loyal to the 'leadership', also threw up their hands in bewilderment. They weren't dissembling either. New clandestine forces have appeared in the NKAR, and are trying to influence public opinion. All the evidence suggests that this is the 'party of Armenian national self-determination', which works underground and has close links with the Armenian diaspora. None of this comes as any surprise. The Karabakh movement, whose intentions are sincere, and which has never proclaimed any aim but the one contained in the brief word 'miatsum' (unification), is being exploited by everyone from the Western press and radio to a rainbow-hued assortment of home-grown radicals.

If it weren't for the deliberate disinformation with which political zealots have been flooding Moscow, central government would have realised long ago that the Karabakh movement was directed against the Soviet authorities only as represented by people like Kevorkov. Authority that was in fact only nominally Soviet. Authority that had progressively stripped the Armenians of every civil right but the right to keep quiet and not make trouble, every privilege but the privilege to be Armenian.

If only the people of Karabakh could have been persuaded to blame their misfortunes not on the Azerbaijanis but on their leaders, degenerate, totalitarian potentates with party cards, as capable as their colleagues in, say, Uzbekistan of telling any lies to keep their power, then perhaps many of these misfortunes might have been averted.

But no! Thanks largely to Kevorkov himself, the movement acquired a very different character. Proud, temperamental people were ultimately forced to respond to the provocations against them. They soon realised that consolidation on nationalist lines proved the firmest and most accessible demand for people in the towns and villages alike, and that slogans for national unity would work perfectly in this situation. So it was that people began attacking each other.

MAFIA OR NO MAFIA?

Konstantin Karlovich Maidanyuk is senior investigator with the Procurator General's serious crimes division. When I met him he was in a thoughtful mood – or probably simply tired: he has been in Nagorno-Karabakh for a long time . . .

'Do you think all this business in the NKAR has been cooked up by the local mafia?' I asked Maidanyuk.

'No, I don't,' he said immediately. 'Or rather that's too simple. We're so used to sticking labels on anything unexpected that it was hard for us at first to make sense of things. A year ago we simply weren't ready for it. But I don't know about the mafia. Can you really imagine a bunch of local crooks and con men organising thousands of people into a desperate political battle in the hope of stirring the mud for a golden fish? So far as I can see, it's just the opposite, and the familiar chain seems to have been broken.'

'So when there's big money around, ethnic differences go out of the window, and the Azerbaijani crook and the Armenian crook get on fine?'

'Exactly. But we're not talking so much about the criminal mafia as the political one,' says Maidanyuk. 'How else to explain the fact, for instance, that the local prosecutor, instead of helping our investigating team from Moscow, did all he could to prevent them getting at the truth? Pressure was put on people who had given evidence to retract it. Everything here is to do with family and social contacts. You're up against a blank wall. And literally everything is bound up with financial relationships. Corruption in the NKAR, as in all the other Soviet regions and republics, is a fact of our economy, and a result of the way local power operates.'

'So how far does this chain of corruption penetrate?'

'In the Autonomous Region, it goes as far as the former First Secretary, Kevorkov himself. And at republic level, to people working in the Azerbaijani government apparatus. I can't name names yet as it's all still *sub judice*, but two of them are of special interest to us in connection with a violent attack on the NKAR prosecutor's office last September.'

'Setting aside the question of national differences, have you any evidence of links between criminal elements in Stepanakert and Baku?'

'Any amount of evidence! Our country's economic administration is still very centralised, with distribution from the top down. The Committee has certainly made some impact in Moscow. But economic plans and their adjustment, material and technical supplies, and financial guarantees are all still fixed by central government. Nothing in the NKAR could be negotiated without bribes, and everything had its price. We have evidence to prove that all conceivable goods and services had – and may still have – their price. A tractor would be 300 roubles, say, and a heavy machine 500. And how did they pay for it? Out of their own pockets? Not on your life! They'd filch raw materials like marble, granite, lime, or what have you, and sell it on the black market for extra cash.'

The main thing I learned from my conversation with Maidanyuk was that the criminal mafia's greatest dream is to merge with the 'politicians': the local bosses of our native 'Cosa Nostra' yearn for political power. They have certainly got quite far already in Armenia, Azerbaijan, and the other republics, and further successes are guaranteed by our inflexible administrative system: bribery and theft are so much easier with the local government and party on your side!

Isn't this why during last spring's demonstrations in Nagorno-Karabakh they stood alongside the compatriots they'd robbed? Isn't this why they repeated their slogans, appeared at their meetings, joined their strikes, and marched on their demonstrations?

But not everything can be bought in the mountains and valleys of this harsh land, and not everything is for sale.

REFUGEES

The Spark Pioneer camp lies within Shusha's city boundaries. There are no smart white shirts and red ties here now, no cheerful drum-beats or bugle-calls. There are plenty of children, though. They've been living here with their parents for some time, and many of them even go to school. They sleep in beds or on the floor, and in the night the older ones keep jumping up to tend the little wood-burning stoves which remind me of ones from my childhood after the war. These are Azerbaijani children.

Running about the corridors of the hotel in Stepanakert and making an incredible din are Armenian children from Shusha. Other little Armenian children staying with their parents in an old students' hostel are more subdued. They are from Sumgait.

These Armenian and Azerbaijani boys and girls – the nation's children, who used to play together in the Pioneer camps – now live apart. I wouldn't mind betting that if you stood two of them together, with their dark hair, dark skins, and large observant eyes, most people wouldn't know which nationality they were. Yet any Armenian three-year-old who has learnt just a few words of its native language will know what 'miatsum' means. And the parents of any three-year-old Azerbaijani will have taught it other words in which to call the Armenians the enemies of Allah and all Azerbaijanis.

But what about the grown-ups . . . ?

Laura Saakovna Arumstyan lived with her family in Dzheiren-batan, on the outskirts of Sumgait. On 27 February last year she and her husband, Andronik, went to collect their daughter-in-law,

Liana, from the Sumgait maternity hospital. At five in the evening great crowds started pouring through the town with portraits on red banners ('Just like May Day, only quieter'), on which they had written 'Death to Armenians!' Laura had to break off her story for a while . . .

They managed by some miracle to escape to her brother's place in Baku, and from there to Stepanakert. ('We're just glad to be alive!')

Guba Tamid Shukurova and her family arrived in Shusha from the village of Saravan in the Azizbekov district of Armenia, where Guba and her friends were milkmaids at the local state farm. After the March events in Sumgait, the women had to be taken to work by a military escort. Then they were advised to get out . . . There are now ten of them – six adults and four children – living in one small room at the Spark Pioneer camp. Half the floorboards are broken, and at night there are rats. ('The medical staff put down poison, but next day they'll be scrabbling away under the floor again!')

Shukurova's husband and daughter both died in Saravan, and she complains only that she cannot visit their graves. No one here complains of anything, glad only to be alive. Others weren't so lucky. 'Take Natik and Zemfira Murtazaev, from the village of Akhta. People surrounded the village and shot at their windows, and everyone fled. They escaped half-naked over the mountain pass in winter, and many of them froze to death . . .'

Laura Arustamyan and Guba Shukurova don't know each other, of course. These two women, who have worked hard all their lives and brought up their children, are guilty of nothing. Yesterday they might have been friends. Today they are enemies.

There are hundreds of thousands of refugees, pouring into the sanatoriums, boarding-houses, and Pioneer camps, or moving in with relatives and turning their flats into Noah's arks. By early morning they're queuing up for work and accommodation, writing collective letters to Moscow and the local capitals to demand justice.

Their bitterness goes very deep, and spills over into mutual recriminations and moral blindness.

'I didn't believe in Allah until the earthquake in Armenia,' a pleasant-looking young man from Shusha said to me at the height of the Muslim holiday of Novruz Bairam. 'But Allah had to punish those non-believers.'

'Aren't you sorry for them?' I asked him, shocked.

'Sure', he said. 'And we even gave blood. But they refused our blood. And now I believe in Allah . . .'

No one wants to be the first to make concessions. The madness of nationalism robs people of all compassion.

Chronicle, 1989
From leaflets distributed in the NKAR
'Our courage is being exploited . . . The strike showed that it's not our common cause that's winning but those who have entered into negotiations with the Russian-Muslim Committee . . .'

'People of Artsakh★ know other time-servers and yes-men who have welcomed this regime of "Special Democratic Repression . . ." This is to warn all the "governors" of Artsakh that Artsakh will not be governed!

Artsakh Front of Miatsum'

'All questions relating to the NKAR are settled on orders from Baku. The scum who grew rich under Kevorkov have raised their heads again. These traitors and toadies now echo what the Committee says . . .

Committee of Artsakh – Armenia'

So the Special Administrative Committee is being attacked from both sides. One side, which signs its leaflets in the name of some probably non-existent unofficial organisations, attacks the 'Russian-Muslim Committee' (sic), while the other describes the Committee as pro-Armenian. Provocations? Undoubtedly, bearing in mind that, according to Arkady Volsky, the Committee wasn't arbitrarily foisted on the two republics 'from above', but was a result of compromise and long discussions between Azerbaijani and Armenian deputies to the USSR Supreme Soviet. The country's leaders acted merely as intermediaries, then law-makers, in the creation of a special administration in Nagorno-Karabakh, and a form of power which would be temporarily acceptable to both sides. Proof of the Committee's popularity is the fact that over *96 per cent* of the electorate in Karabakh voted for Volsky as people's deputy at the national Supreme Soviet elections on 26 March. No one made them. The elections were as democratic here as everywhere else in the Soviet Union.

★Artsakh is the Armenian name for Nagorno-Karabakh.

Fate has decreed that I should witness a brief moment of this country's age-old history. Every week has brought new facts from one side or the other, new evidence of the tragic conflict between two ancient nations whose history is so intertwined, who have lived together for centuries, and who will surely do so again.

What will happen now?

Objectively speaking, the Committee is the first rational step towards political stabilisation in the region. This is the view shared by progressive opinion both here and abroad. But there can be few local leaders nowadays who have such a hard time of it as these committee members, experienced politicians trying to carry out intelligent, sensitive policies. They're balanced on a knife-edge, and like sappers they can't afford to make mistakes.

The Committee has done more for Nagorno-Karabakh in two months than the old party leaders did in several years. They have set in process regional self-financing in Nagorno-Karabakh, complete economic independence for its enterprises, and the revival of traditional branches of Karabakh agriculture, such as vine-growing. New structural reforms in the NKAR will allow the region to be more effectively administered, and its decaying, semi-feudal inequalities will become a thing of the past. Arkady Volsky recently announced that the pompous palace built by Kevorkov as a House of Culture will be handed over to children.

But it will be a long haul. One can understand central government's impatience to get results, and to 'resolve' all questions overnight. This might at first appear possible. But once one arrives in Stepanakert it immediately becomes clear that it isn't. Nothing will change overnight. To end the state of emergency now and disband the Committee would be to invite new violence between the two peoples. We must be under no illusions about this; it is the soldiers who maintain order in the Special Region now, and people here beg them not to leave.

They won't leave. Not yet . . . But does this mean that an acceptable form of permanent administration can only be found when tensions are at white heat? This doesn't bear thinking about. The people of Karabakh live in hope.

Before leaving Stepanakert I recorded on my dictaphone a song which was born on the square at the height of last year's meetings and has become very popular. It was composed by a simple Karabakhite who had never written anything before. The whole square sang it after him, and now every child and old person knows it. 'Brothers and sisters!' sings a defenceless child's voice. 'All Armenia is with us. We won't turn back. Armenians we'll remain.' I was surprised to discover that this song has now been virtually banned, but it is nonetheless sung in every house and played on every tape-player.

If we're serious about creating a genuinely legal democratic system, we must ensure that no one has the power to rob one nation of the right to decide its own fate.

It's easy to be wise with hindsight. Must we wait for another Sumgait in another part of the country? Can the situation be brought under control before it reaches crisis-point? Or does the proper settlement of national disputes exclude compromises? Finally, why have we not yet named those individuals hitherto protected by their power, who tried to steer the Karabakh movement off-course, and were the chief cause of all the disasters that ensued?

For too long we have stumbled on blindly, listening to hymns to the 'indestructible friendship between brotherly nations'. Then shooting broke out in Alma Ata, the Crimean Tatars took to the streets, and events unfolded in Nagorno-Karabakh. For too long we have been surrounded by the stereotypes bequeathed to us by Stalin. Now the myths are shattering, with endless inevitable bloody tragedies. To keep silent about this means to multiply the misfortunes of the innocent people of our common homeland, who will always ultimately pay for the mistakes of others.

It is now time for us to speak.

The 'Lokhankin Phenomenon' and the Russian Intelligentsia
Vyacheslav Kostikov

The author traces the destruction of the Soviet intelligentsia from the trials of the 'Miners' and the 'Industrialists', charged with receiving money from the West to wreck Soviet industry, to Stalin's description of intellectuals as a weak-willed 'stratum', presided over in the 1940s by his cultural henchman, Nikolai Zhdanov.

There's a certain grim pleasure to be had from scanning the records of the Rehabilitation Commission for the virtually forgotten names of the insulted and the injured. But this doesn't lessen the need to understand this tragic paradox of Soviet history: that the Revolution, created by generations of Russian intellectuals and universally ac-knowledged to have given the country the most educated govern-ment in the world, should within ten years have turned against its own creators.

We would need to immerse ourselves in our official history books to grasp the full contempt in which the nation's leaders have held this intellectual 'stratum'. Literature, theatre, and film all gradually absorbed the image of the snivelling, wavering ninny, terrified of the Revolution and hostile to the working class. This image was closely based on that of the Menshevik or the Socialist Revolutionary, who became even more closely identified as 'enemies of the people'. And as the prestige of the intelligentsia declined, scientific literature too gave weighty support to the notion of its counter-revolutionary nature.

Practically all the trials of the thirties, regardless of whom they were fabricated against – the Trotskyists, the 'Right and Left Deviationists', the 'Industrialists', the 'Miners', and so on – were essentially trials against creative thought, and the need for intellectual work was admitted only through clenched teeth: *someone* had to invent machines, build planes, and make advances in science.

The artificial alienation of ordinary working people from the intelligentsia became increasingly apparent. In his book *Self-Knowledge*, the philosopher Nikolai Berdyaev recalls that when the All-Russian Union of Writers (a professional, non-party organisation) had to register itself in the early twenties, writing was not seen as belonging to any existing category of labour, and the union was finally registered as a branch of the print-workers' union.

People born into the intelligentsia had their access to higher education blocked, and were sentenced to gradual intellectual extinction. Fears that the intelligentsia would 'pollute' the revolutionary class with their corrupt ideology and morality led to harsh restrictions on party membership. The younger generation were increasingly offered new heroes to emulate, such as Cheka agents, Voroshilov's Red Guards, and Budyonny's cavalrymen, and fewer and fewer writers, artists, and scientists.

Stalin's suspicion of the intelligentsia meant that with each successive government shake-up the number of intellectuals in it declined. This naturally meant that politics (including the politics of culture, science, and art) was increasingly defined by people who regarded culture as the last thing a leader needed.

It wasn't simply a matter of educational qualifications: these could always be bought, as happened in a number of the Soviet republics, where people in the government only had to ingratiate themselves in the right academic circles for degrees and diplomas to fall into their laps. No, it was rather a matter of the general collapse of the power of culture.

Some people will point to the 'Leninist tradition' in working-class politics. But in Lenin's day the very notion of the party member was different from that in the decades that followed. In those days the party's vanguard consisted overwhelmingly of intellectuals and educated workers. Research carried out in 1924 by the Party Central Committee reveals that the majority of leading party workers were from the intelligentsia. At this time 93.3 per cent of those working in the Commissariat of Education were intellectuals, as well as 76.6 per cent of those in the Central Executive Committee and the government, 69.7 per cent of those in the Finance Commissariat, and 63.2 per cent of all provincial executive committee presidents.

Naturally both local and central government was more flexible in those days, capable of assessing its own mistakes and correcting them accordingly. Witness the whole attitude to collaboration with the West, exemplified by the New Economic Policy and the Genoa Conference in 1922, in which the Soviet Union sought some sort of *modus vivendi* with Europe.

Yet after Lenin's death, the Stalin era was launched with mass 'appeals' to join the party, in which the concepts of party member and intellectual appeared to be almost mutually exclusive.

By 1925 there were already some 30,000 party members who were totally illiterate, and doubtless a far larger number who were functionally illiterate. The majority of delegates to the 16th Party Conference in 1930 had only a primary education, or a partial secondary education. Here, then, was that malleable mass which with a little warmth could be moulded into whatever shape was required. The party's immunity to ignorance and blind obedience was thus drastically weakened, along with its members' capacity for independent creative thought and political action. The purpose of this policy was crystal clear: to transform the party from the collective of the nation's brains and vanguard into an obedient tool in the power struggle, which would automatically lend its support to the dictatorship.

Stalin ruthlessly pursued this goal. Declaring himself to be Lenin's heir and disciple, his attitude to the intellectuals was in fact far more reminiscent of that of the Polish socialist J. W. Machaiski, who at the turn of the century articulated a brand of anti-intellectualism which regarded the 'brain-worker' as the enemy of the proletarian class. Machaiski's shadow hovered over the Soviet intelligentsia for many decades to come, and however hard Khrushchev attempted to distance himself from Stalin, he could not overcome these suspicions. He merely made an exception for the 'technocrats', knowing full well that his slogan 'Catch up with and outstrip America' couldn't be made to work without a technological intelligentsia.

Our present backwardness in many fields of science and technology, along with the degradation of our economy and our social sciences, is the price we are now paying for the anti-intellectualism of the Stalin, Khrushchev, and Brezhnev eras. It wasn't the October Revolution that slowed down the development of culture in Russia. Despite the devastating civil war which followed it, and the virtual disappearance of canvas, marble, paper, and so on, Russia experienced a great surge of creative energy in those years. 'In her most difficult days Russia was like an orchard of nightingales,' wrote the poet Andrei Bely then. 'There was no strength left in us, yet we all burst into song.'

The tragedy of the Russian intelligentsia was not that it had no bread or paints, but that history deformed and castrated its essential meaning and purpose: its freedom of thought, its independence from official authority, its participation in world culture, its cultural and spiritual internationalism, its non-adherence to dogma.

The start of this attack on the intelligentsia may be traced from 1922, when Lenin was too ill actively to oppose the bureaucratisation of government and intellectual life. A *Pravda* article published in that year, 'Dictatorship, Where Is Thy Whip?', signed with the mysterious letter 'O' (some have speculated that this may have been Trotsky), launched the persecution of those intellectuals who still defended their right to hold opinions independent of the prevailing ideology. The article was followed by practical measures to 'purge' the country of its critics. In August 1922, 160 people – the first Soviet 'dissidents' – were expelled to Germany by order of the GPU.

Most of these 'troublemakers' were university teachers, journalists, philosophers, doctors, agricultural economists, and organisers of co-operatives. In order to play down the negative impact of this mass expulsion, it was explained that they were all 'ideological White Guard supporters of Kolchak and Wrangel', and that there weren't any big names amongst them.

In fact those expelled included Novikov, the rector of Moscow University and professor of zoology; Professor Karsavin, the rector of Petrograd University; a group of mathematicians headed by Professor Stratonov, deacon of Moscow's mathematics faculty; several eminent economists, co-operative organisers, and historians; the sociologist Pitirim Sorokin; and the famous idealist philosophers Berdyaev, Frank, Lossky, Vysheslavtsev, Ilin, Trubetskoy, and Bulgakov.

The true horror of this mass expulsion of dissident intellectuals was not that it robbed the country of so many great brains, for Russia still remained rich in brains. Its purpose was not so much to punish the intelligentsia as to warn and frighten them. Hence the title of another *Pravda* article about the expulsion, 'The First Warning'.

It did indeed achieve its purpose. All the things Evgeny Zamyatin warned us about in his novel *We* – the personality degraded into a number, and the intellect into an appendage of the Single State headed by the Benefactor – gradually became a nightmarish reality. The veteran writer V. Veresaev, who had wholeheartedly embraced the Revolution, put it this way: 'We cannot be ourselves. Our artistic conscience is constantly being violated. Our writing becomes increasingly two-tiered – one for publication, the other for ourselves.'

Only Maxim Gorky could still speak out, and in 1922 he protested sharply against the trial of the Socialist Revolutionaries, appealing to Anatole France and Lenin's deputy Alexei Rykov to intervene on their behalf.

'I beg you to inform L. D. Trotsky and others,' Gorky wrote to Rykov, 'that these are my views. They should come as no surprise to you, since a thousand times during the Revolution I have pointed out to the Soviet authorities the criminal senselessness of destroying the intelligentsia in this illiterate and uncultured country of ours. I am now convinced that if the SRs are killed, this action will provoke socialist Europe to a moral blockade of Russia.'

A moral blockade was indeed created, but only years later, after evidence of Stalin's foul crimes had started filtering through to Europe. This finally exhausted revolutionary Russia's vast moral credit in the eyes of the Western intelligentsia, and the moral blockade, followed by the political blockade, drove us to yet more monstrous acts . . .

The tragedy of the Russian intelligentsia can be clearly seen in Gorky's own life. Returning to Moscow in 1928, he was soon forced to abide by certain 'rules'. In order to retain some of his authority to defend Russian and Soviet culture, he started living by his wits and making bitter compromises with his conscience. Having spent years defending the innocent, he participated in the cooked-up trial of the 'Industrialists', by accusing the defendants even before the trial opened of being involved in a counter-revolutionary plot. In partial defence of Gorky, we may say that he did not know the truth and sincerely believed the accusations. Yet he could scarcely have failed to see the forced labour of the thousands of prisoners who built the Belomor Baltic Canal. In his letters from there to foreign friends, however, he denied that part of the grandiose edifice of socialism was being constructed by convict labour, and he collaborated in possibly the most shameful cover-up in the history of Soviet journalism, praising the labour feats of the Gulag by suggesting that the work of the Cheka agents in the camps was clear proof of the proletariat's 'humanism'.

What could one expect from people who didn't have Gorky's fame to protect them?

As violence and lies permeated our entire social life, the intelligentsia was remorselessly drawn into its greatest crime of all – servility – and its already ephemeral hope of any dignified collaboration with the authorities was finally dashed.

'Fellow-travellers' still ventured a kind of polemic in the literary journal *Red Virgin Soil*, under the protection of its editor, the old Bolshevik Alexander Voronsky. These non-proletarian intellectuals meanwhile still had a few defenders left in the Party Central Committee, headed by Bukharin. Bukharin's ironic response to leaders of the All-Russian Association of Proletarian Writers, who demanded the immediate establishment of a proletarian intellectual dictatorship, was 'first learn to read and write, then learn to wash your hands'.

At a conference of the Moscow committee of the party in 1925, Academician P. Sakulin declared in the name of those intellectuals prepared to co-operate with Soviet power that 'no one has a monopoly on the truth . . . whose very existence demands freedom of teaching, research, and scientific competition'. But Sakulin's words already rang out too boldly, and were to be one of the Russian intelligentsia's last suicidal bursts of courage. Most were already growing accustomed to the bitter fact that the last remnants of freedom couldn't survive without cruel self-censorship and endless genuflections to the authorities.

The intelligentsia now appeared ready to accept its inadequacy and bare its neck for the inevitable blows. 'We non-party intellectuals, and even those walking firmly in step with Soviet power, cannot now be given our full political freedom in case we say too much,' declared O. Klyuchinsky, a former member of Changing Landmarks, a group of writers and academics formed in 1920 to defend the high calling and social responsibility of the intelligentsia. According to the stenographic records, the new intellectuals assembled in the Great Hall of the Moscow Conservatoire greeted Klyuchinsky's declaration with cheers and applause.

He was not alone in his self-flagellation. P. Kogan, a well-known literary critic of the 1920s, did not simply genuflect to the authorities, but demanded that 'dreams of freedom be banished, so that discipline is not weakened. The new revolution has brought us a splendid new yoke, not a gilded yoke, but a solid, well-constructed iron one. This is the only path to liberation. Those who do not understand this understand nothing of present events.'

The Russian intelligentsia, tracing its evolution from Radishchev, Novikov, and Chaadaev, no longer existed, for true intellectuals cannot glorify their own subordination. Crazed and terrified, they now appeared to their readers as sex-obsessed scroungers, lounging on the sofa in braces and green socks. Could Ilf and Petrov have guessed, when they created their Vasisual Lokhankin, the intellectual smashed to a pulp by his communal flat-mates for not switching off the lavatory light, that concealed beneath all the sniggering analyses of 'Lokhankin and his role in the Russian Revolution', or 'Lokhankin and the Tragedy of Russian Liberalism', lay the real tragedy of the intellectuals, beaten to a pulp by the vast communal barracks which was now our country, and then going down on their knees to thank their persecutors?

'Perhaps this is right and proper,' thinks Lokhankin, shuddering under the blows and staring at the armour-plated toenails on his tormentor's feet. 'Perhaps this is the path to redemption and purification . . .'

The real tragedy of the former intelligentsia was that its fate was now decided by Nikita Pryakhin, a retired janitor with armour-plated toenails, who yelled at the top of his voice: 'We can do whatever we want!'

Under the lash of all these retired janitors and generals with whom our culture was now so generously endowed, the intelligentsia finally turned itself into a mass production line. Bukharin himself even cast this vivid phrase into the darkness: 'Yes, we can put our stamp on the intellectuals and manufacture them as in a factory.' Poets immediately seized on this metaphor, trilling it out like nightingales in every conceivable key. It wasn't only the worst or the most pliant of them who did so either. Witness I. Selvinsky: 'Think of us, comrades, switch on our nerves, and work us like machines in a factory!' Or I. Utkin: 'We are fuel for your smelting furnace.' Stalin, of course, found a much larger smelting furnace for the intelligentsia: the Gulag Archipelago.

In 1929 Alexander Voronsky was arrested for defending the 'fellow-travellers', and that autumn marked the start of the persecution of Pilnyak and Zamyatin. The choice of these two writers was no accident: the first was president of the Moscow Writers' Union, the second was president of the union's Leningrad branch. The authorities went straight to the top, and their aim was the same as it had been when they expelled the intellectuals in 1922: to smash the 'ringleaders' and intimidate the others. The victims must be made examples of. All must be made to understand that the government could destroy whoever they wanted, whenever they wanted, without asking anyone's permission.

There was no political opposition left. The moral opposition, represented by Gorky, had been neutralised. The fellow-travellers were finished, redundant. All that were needed now were yes-men, who like the poet Sashka Ryukhina, in Bulgakov's *The Master and Margarita*, could hammer out verses on the theme of 'soar up, and soar away . . .'

In 1937 they got the last ones – not fellow-travellers but their own people, those who had lived body and soul for the Revolution and had welcomed and approved of everything it did, but had made the mistake of shyly mentioning their desire to be themselves and their right to their own likes and dislikes. By now, however, any mention of 'artistic integrity' was regarded as dangerous heresy. Protesting against the persecutions, the writers of the Crossing group spoke of the need to create a 'public opinion that is not afraid of writers'. After Yezhov became head of the NKVD in 1936, this was considered tantamount to an attack on Stalin's secret police, and the members of the group – Ivan Kataev, Boris Guber, Nikolai Zarudin, Abram Lezhnev, and Boris Pilnyak – were arrested. Zarudin was shot. Kataev got twenty years in a camp, Guber got fifteen, and Lezhnev, according to the evidence, died under interrogation. Pilnyak was last seen in 1939 in the Bear Mountain concentration camp where the author of *The Tale of the Unextinguished Moon* was felling trees.

In Dostoyevsky's *The Devils*, Shchigalyov spelt out his programme thus: 'Those who are most gifted are ostracised or put to death. They gouge out Copernicus' eyes, cut out Cicero's tongue, throw stones at Shakespeare . . .'

The writers of the Crossing group weren't geniuses, they merely wanted to serve the people modestly within the limits of their talent. But Stalin's ideological zealots went much further than Shchigalyov. For them even average talents were dangerous. And so violence and soullessness spread their grey wings over the vast expanse of one-sixth of the earth's surface.

The spiritual life of the country was now completely monopolised by the Single State. Endless rules and edicts dictated the course of music, ballet, cinema, song, and above all literature. Even sport was subjected to this ideological overhaul. 'Now is the time to put an end once and for all to neutrality in chess,' declared chess connoisseur and People's Commissar of Justice Krylenko, already noted in 1932 for his role as accuser in several political trials. 'We must organise shock brigades of chess-players, and pledge ourselves to a Five-year plan in chess!'

The completion of collectivisation in 1932 saw the completion of yet another process, fraught with dire consequences: the collectivisation of consciousness, intellect, and talent. That year saw the formation of a single union of Soviet writers, and other groups of the intelligentsia soon followed them in taking the oath of allegiance.

The collectivisation of the intelligentsia, its loss of all rights but the right to sing the praises of its leaders and their 'achievements', completed the deformation of socialism in Russia, whose source and inspiration had been that very same Russian intelligentsia, as represented by Plekhanov, Lenin, and a whole dazzling galaxy of revolutionaries. The collectivisation of intellect involved the manufacture of as many lies as the usurping leadership needed to maintain itself in power. It marked the start of decades of terror and long years of falsehood, which continued until 1985.

In concluding these melancholy notes on the fate of the Russian and Soviet intelligentsia, I should like to quote from that great early nineteenth-century martyr to the cause of Russian spirituality, Pyotr Chaadaev, arrested and declared insane for his liberal views: 'We have no power now over the past, but the future depends on us.' If our future is to differ from the evil dreams of the Zhdanovs and the Suslovs, we must understand the causes of the ruin into which our country collapsed, and with it the intelligentsia.

From time immemorial Russia has maintained a passionate faith in the power of truth. To attain this truth we must now ponder upon our own history and fate.

> Are we guilty if your skeleton snaps
> In our heavy, gentle hands?

Yes, we are guilty!
We are guilty of separating socialism from democracy. Guilty of

obliterating freedom from our concept of socialism. Guilty of allowing the totalitarian lie to overshadow the truth of Communism. Guilty of trampling on the individual in pursuit of the chimera of greatness. Guilty of distorting the meaning and purpose of the Socialist Revolution.

Does this mean then that the Socialist Revolution was a historical mistake?

The philosopher Nikolai Berdyaev (maligned in all the history books by Zhdanov's henchmen) pointed to the tragedy of the Revolution, but emphasised too that a revolution in Russia could only be a socialist one, although the Russian spiritual temperament made it possible that it would also be a totalitarian one. But be all this as it may, he wrote, 'the Russian Revolution has unleashed the mighty forces of the Russian people. That is its chief meaning!'

The present growth in our cultural and moral life started the moment the first fetters of fear were loosed, and is proof that our spiritual well-springs are not exhausted. Nor is the memory of culture. It once seemed as though the deadening currents of 'Zhdanov's fluid' had obliterated the cultural 'strata' bearing the names of our most honourable intellectuals. But the moment we stayed the hand of the ideological usurpers, memory began shyly, and then ever more boldly, to whisper the names of the martyrs to truth: Platonov, Pasternak, Florensky, Bulgakov, Bukharin, Rozanov, Zamyatin, Pilnyak, Filonov, Fydorov, Vavilov, Shalamov, Chayanov . . .

The inveterate toadies are still with us, of course, along with the professional augurers who proclaimed the Brezhnevite 'renewal'. But now there is a yearning to be rid of the slave within us. The path from slavery to freedom is neither simple nor short, but it is already visible. The foundations of our rightful future government are now being cleansed of their accumulation of false formulae and intimidating decrees. And in these mighty labours the revived well-springs of the intelligentsia must join with the 'great forces of the Russian people' which were awakened by the Socialist Revolution.

A Haunting Spectre
Natalya Ilina

The journal Our Contemporary *is one of the bastions of Soviet reaction, closely identified with the nationalistic, quasi-fascistic groups which seek to undermine perestroika and glasnost. It recently published a sensational novel entitled* Judgement Day, *in which an American agent infiltrates Soviet society and successfully subverts it. The crude way in which all our political failures are blamed on the Jews and the 'sinister forces of reaction' carries echoes of the paranoia of the Stalin era.*

The recent emergence of fascism in the Soviet Union demonstrates the frightening speed at which the mythical 'Protocols of Zion' can be carried on to the streets in times of crisis. This new Soviet fascism traces its origins back to the Russian émigré circles of the 1930s. All of which takes the author back to her own youth in the Manchurian town of Harbin.

In 1931 the Japanese marched into Manchuria. The following February they occupied Harbin, where they were welcomed by the Russian Fascist Party, founded and led by Konstantin Rodzaevsky, former aide-in-chief to the exiled anti-Bolshevik leader Ataman Semyonov.

Rodzaevsky's Harbin fascists were financially supported by the Japanese military police and espionage mafias, who in their turn used the fascists for their own criminal purposes. The drug trade flourished, gambling dens sprang up, and many fascists got jobs in the Japanese-controlled police force, which systematically raided the houses of Soviet citizens employed by the Chinese Eastern Railway, on the pretext that they were Communist sympathisers or 'Comintern agents'.

In the spring of 1933 my uncle, the botanist A. Voeikov, set off over the river Sungara to collect plants, and didn't return. We soon learned that he had been kidnapped by the Chinese bandits known as the Khunkhuzy, who demanded an enormous sum of money for his release. The Harbin newspapers demanded that the Japanese punish the kidnappers, but people tended to disappear almost as a matter of course in those days and no one was terribly surprised. Their usual targets were rich and generally Jewish, whereas we were just poor powerless immigrants. But they also made mistakes, and this is what had happened in the case of my uncle, who had evidently been mistaken for someone else.

Having realised their mistake, they reduced their ransom demand, and Uncle was eventually returned to us for 500 yen.

But before this, Mother went to see Konstantin Nakamura.

Nakamura was a russified Japanese and an important person in the Japanese police force. From there he maintained links between the police and the Russian fascists, and he was also the brains behind the Khunkhuzy.

He explained to my mother, in impeccable Russian, that the Japanese army was much too busy to chase up the Khunkhuzy, that it would be unwise to trifle with them, and that she had better pay up. She went straight back to our boarding-house and organised a lottery, and by the autumn we had got Uncle back.

Meanwhile the Russian Fascist Party flourished. People would cross the street at the sight of these young men in their belted black shirts, high boots, and swastika arm-bands, who greeted each other by throwing out their right arm with the words 'Glory to Russia!' They had their own club too, with a huge swastika on the roof and a gambling den on the first floor. The building was on the main street, almost next door to Harbin's most expensive hotel, and copies of their newspaper, *Our Road*, were prominently displayed on plywood hoardings throughout the town. Between the words 'Our' and 'Road' was a small swastika topped by a two-headed eagle, and one would catch glimpses of headlines such as 'World Conspiracy of Jews and Masons', and 'Russia for the Russians!'

All articles were signed 'Co. Ziberg', or 'Co. Martynov', or 'Co. Rodzaevsky'. The abbreviation stood for 'companion-in-arms', and this was how they addressed one another. Hitler was their god, Mussolini their idol.

This is what happens when people with neither literary skills nor imagination are carried away by some idea, but are unable to express themselves.

None of this can be said of Rodzaevsky, the fascists' 'Führer'. A well-read man who loved music, Rodzaevsky was the stuff of which fanatics are made, possessed by a single burning passion: his hatred of the Jews. This was the subject of all his writings and all his speeches at the fascist club. He was said to be a great natural orator in the hysterical mould, whose audiences were apt to rush out on to the streets to put his words into practice.

One night the windows of the synagogue would be smashed; then a gang of black-shirts would carry out a pogrom in Goldstein's haberdashery . . . But I don't suppose the young louts responsible were punished too severely, for they suited the mafia's purpose perfectly.

Unlike Rodzaevsky, Nakamura had no strong feelings about Jews and cared only about money, and since most Jewish people in Harbin lived in the same poverty as the rest of us Russian refugees he took no interest in them. There were, however, some rich Jews too.

One of these was a jeweller named Iosif Kaspe. Every evening the window of Kaspe's shop would be covered with a steel grille, but by day the Sèvres porcelain, the jewels and the Fabergé rabbits would sparkle on their blue velvet, enticing in everyone who passed. Nakamura couldn't bear it.

In the summer of 1933, Kaspe was visited by his younger son, a pianist, who had just graduated from the Paris Conservatoire and gave a number of concerts in Harbin. It was at one of these concerts that I heard for the first time the music of Debussy, whose 'Jardins sous la pluie' made a very deep impression on me. I can still see that youthful figure with his sharp profile and delicate fingers, the folds of his frock coat falling from the stool. The clarity of the image was sharpened by the horror of what followed.

Young Kaspe was kidnapped by the Khunkhuzy, who ordered his father to pay a ransom of 300,000 dollars. Old Kaspe indignantly refused, and a month later he received a neatly wrapped cardboard box containing his son's chopped-off ears. Young Kaspe never returned, and shortly afterwards his father received a coffin containing his dismembered body.

I didn't attend the funeral, but I read about the 'Kaspe affair' in the newspapers, and was as horrified as everyone else.

As life in Manchuria became increasingly intolerable, more and more of us started to leave. Throughout the 1930s, Russian émigrés poured into China, and at the end of 1936 we escaped to Shanghai.

On 9 August 1945 the Soviet Union declared war on Japan. After Japan's defeat, Soviet troops marched into Harbin, and we who had lived there had no doubt that the fascists there would now pay for their crimes.

Rodzaevsky and some of his associates managed to escape to China before the Soviet troops arrived, and they settled in Tientsin. From here they heard of the ecstatic welcome the Harbin émigrés had given the occupying Soviet troops. Shortly afterwards, the names of Rodzaevsky's 'companions-in-arms' started appearing in the newspapers. The world over which the 'Russian Führer' had presided for almost two decades was in ruins.

Rodzaevsky learned that his 'blood brother', Ataman Semyonov, had held a banquet in Dairen in honour of the Soviet commanders, and had then left for Moscow. What Rodzaevsky didn't know, though, was that the moment Semyonov arrived he was packed off to the Lubyanka and hanged. Rodzaevsky reasoned that the Ataman was already old, whereas he was still in the prime of life, wasting away with nothing to do. Meanwhile his 'companions' in Tientsin had been picking up rumours that the victors were magnanimous and that everyone who sincerely admitted their mistakes and wanted to work for their country would be forgiven.

Homesickness made Rodzaevsky long to believe these rumours, and he composed two letters, one to Marshal Malinovsky and one to Stalin.

At this point a charming young official from the Soviet consulate in Peking arrived in Tientsin and introduced himself to Rodzaevsky. He made a delightful impression on him, saying all the things the former 'Führer' longed to hear. Their country needed people with his energy, experience, and talent, he said. During the war we had suffered enormous losses, and the Anglo-American imperialists could easily exploit this . . .

These words were guaranteed to enrage Rodzaevsky, linked as they were in his fevered brain with the 'Mason-Jews'. He vowed to his congenial guest to fight this enemy under any banner. The official then assured him that his country had a high regard for his political and journalistic experience. He would have to act quickly, however, for he had many enemies in Tientsin.

So Rodzaevsky left for Peking. He was given a splendid apartment in the Soviet consulate there, but was warned not to leave the building for his own safety.

In the ensuing days of silence, solitude, and reflection, Rodzaevsky sat for hours at his desk, writing and rewriting his letters to Malinovsky and Stalin.

He had made many mistakes in his life, Rodzaevsky wrote to Stalin, all because it had taken him so long to grasp the simple fact that Iosif Stalin was the leader Russia needed, who had brought order to his country, led it to victory, and extended its borders.

To be sure, Rodzaevsky had worked for the Japanese in the hope that they would cleanse Russia of Communists. And yes, he had supported Germany during the war, believing that Hitler would rid Russia of the Jews. Yet all along he had sought Russia's salvation from outside, and had overlooked the main thing: the wisdom of her leader! Rodzaevsky was now sure that Stalin understood that the Jews were Russia's most dangerous enemy, and would tackle once and for all the pernicious 'Jewish question'.

'We have gradually come to the conclusion that Stalinism is identical to what we used to call "Russian fascism",' he concluded. 'Stalinism is our own native Russian fascism, purged of extremes, illusions, and misconceptions.'

He wrote on, pausing to gaze out of the window at the desolate autumnal garden below. 'I am willing to accept all responsibility for the activities of the Russian Fascist Party,' he wrote. Then feverishly changing his mind, he added: 'I want to start a new life, as a national Communist and convinced Stalinist!'

Shortly afterwards Rodzaevsky's solitary life came to an end, and he was flown to Moscow, where he was taken to the Lubyanka, tried, and shot.

'Count' Anastase Vonsyatsky, leader of the Russian Fascist National Revolutionary Party in America, also had some very flattering things to say about Stalin in 1939. And what was it about Iosif Vissarionovich that so pleased Vonsyatsky? The fact that he had 'destroyed more Communists than Hitler, Mussolini, and Chiang Kai-shek put together'.

But we should not deceive ourselves that fascists like Rodzaevsky and Vonsyatsky only operate abroad. Hard though it may be to admit, there is a certain inevitability about their reappearance throughout history. Every generation over the past century has suffered to some extent from this disorder. In times of transition and turmoil, when the old façades collapse and new vistas appear, people flounder about in search of certainty, and cling to the first piece of firm ground they find.

Judgement Day's talk of 'sinister forces' and its far-fetched episodes of psychological warfare are merely presenting the readers of *Our Contemporary* with a reanimated and prettified version of the 'Protocols of Zion'. It may be very soothing in these uncertain times to blame outside forces for our misfortunes. But to identify the 'enemy' in this way encourages the illusion of a system that is beyond change or criticism. If this was *Our Contemporary*'s intention in publishing the novel, they have surely succeeded.

Matryona's Crime
Ilya Kartushin and Special correspondent Zamira Ibrahimova

The party has recently issued a decree 'On the Restoration of Justice to the Victims of the Repressions of the 1930s, 1940s, and early 1950s'. The machine of repression, created, installed, and operated by the state in those tragic years, relied heavily on its informers. How did this happen?

Let us consider the story of an unknown peasant woman named Matryona Chuchalina, born ninety years ago this year. Few people can celebrate such a long life, and sinful Matryona had a hard job surviving amongst her blameless compatriots, who regarded their 'denunciation' of her as a conscientious service to the state.

We must now release Matryona Chuchalina from her great crime, and beg her and her descendants' forgiveness for the delirium that descended on her.

We discovered her case amongst countless similar cases in the archives of the Novosibirsk provincial court. These piles of tattered grey files, bearing the ominous mauve stamp 'Accused under Article, 58/10, Clause 2 of the Criminal Code', evidently belonged to another department, authorised to guard state security.* But by some lucky chance here they were, thousands of stories of ordinary human crimes, three dozen files containing the fates of 'political' criminals.

No celebrities here, not one marshal, party activist, theatre director, or poet. Just a weaver named Ulyanova Erokhina, a blacksmith named Mitrofan Artamonov, and a Siberian collective-farm worker named Matryona Chuchalina. Not one imposing name or 'show trial'. Alongside all the big names are these 'rank-and-file subver-

---

*Article 58/10 of the Criminal Code made it an imprisonable offence to 'organise or spread propaganda against the Soviet system'.

sives', whose fate was the camps, the prisons, a crown of thorns, and a remote, anonymous grave.

What did these 'little folk' do to deserve such treatment?

Matryona's case consists of sixty-eight documents. The investigation started on 17 June 1941 and ended on 10 March 1942. Sentence was delivered on 22 June 1942.

It was the first terrible year of the war. The entire staff at many frontier posts had been slaughtered. The Nazis had seized Latvia, Lithuania, parts of Estonia, most of the Ukraine, and almost all Byelorussia and Moldavia, were plunging into the western regions of the Russian Federation, emerging at the approaches to Leningrad, and threatening Smolensk and Kiev.

The Soviet Union was in mortal danger.

Meanwhile deep in the Siberian hinterland, the investigation, the prosecution, and innumerable servants of the Law were busy day and night for eleven months tracking down a simple peasant woman from the Novostroika collective farm. Why was the state so afraid of this illiterate, passportless woman who couldn't even sign her name on the minutes of her own interrogation?

Before the interrogation, however, came the denunciation. Under the number 2 in the prosecution documents is inserted a small scrap of paper (in all documents the original style and spelling have been left as they are) which reads:

> To the Investigator of Kuznets district from Maria Nikolaevna Korevina.
> Statement.
> On 8-VI-1941 Matryona Chuchalina said to some women on the field lets get rid of soviet power then we can all pray to god again. It was Anastasia Manakhova told me. And Maria Sarina, and Ekaterina Melnikova.
>
> 16/VII-1941

And that's it. These few lines are all we have from Matryona's accuser, since Korevina makes no further appearance in the case. The undoubted effectiveness of her laconic 'statement' – the crime is defined, the witnesses named – suggests that she was experienced in the rules of this game. As to her motives, we can only speculate: maybe Matryona and Maria had been in love with the same man, or had had a quarrel, or their children had been in a fight, or else the literate Maria had decided to do the dirty on the unenlightened Matryona in an outburst of civic indignation.

Case 27 provides us with no answer to these questions, but it demonstrates with lethal clarity the power of denunciation in those days.

Document No 1 reads:

> On the 17th day of July, 1941, A. M. Sesov, People's Investigator of the Kuznets district, having taken into account, from the accusation of M. I. Korevina, that citizen Matryona Chuchalina, living at the Novostroika collective farm, in the village of Zhernov, is engaged in counter-revolutionary agitation amongst the farm-workers, has therefore resolved, in accordance with Art. 91 of the Criminal Code:
>
> To start criminal proceedings against Citizen Chuchalina according to Article 58/10, Clause 2 of the Criminal Code of the RSFSR.
>
> People's Investigator Sesov

This is followed by the brisk signature of the prosecutor, Shadrin: 'agreed'.

No more than twenty-four hours after the investigator has met the accuser, the machine of persecution is in full swing. An enemy has been rooted out, there's work to do. And hard work it is, too! On the same day, 17 July, investigator Sesov questions seven witnesses, receives an assessment of Matryona's character from the collective-farm chairman, interrogates the accused, writes three statements, including one on the various available methods of punishment and one on the appointment of expert psychiatric witnesses.

Twelve documents, all dating from the day after the denunciation.

What could be the reason for all this frantic activity? Perhaps the investigator had been hanging around with nothing to do and was happy that something had finally turned up. Perhaps, on the contrary, there was so much work, and Matryona's guilt was so self-evident, that he needed only a day to decide her fate. Perhaps Matryona's case enticed him with the prospect of easy success. Or perhaps heads had to roll, and heads must therefore be found.

He had his pal the informer, anyway. He couldn't have got far without her. Informer and investigator were the kingpins in the chain that was finally to squeeze the life out of Matryona.

Korevina had penned her denunciation, and Sesov had fallen on it with extraordinary official zeal. These were the first two, but by no means the last.

Document 3. caracter asesment of Matryona Chuchalina, of the Novostroika collective farm, Zhernov vilage, Kuznetsk district, declares:

Until 1933 Chuchalina farmed her own land. Because of the religous atitudes of the pesants, Novostroika did not enter the masive colectivisatons of 1929 to 1932. It took part in 1933. Chuchalina had a bad atitude to her work until 1941, and worked less than 100 working days a year, always giving the exuse of her many children . . .

Signed Chairman Bedarkov and Acountant Monakhov

Of Matryona's husband we know only that he 'worked well', unlike Matryona, who was 'always poring out her disatisfaction'.

These two writers were very anxious to please the investigator. Despite the atrocious spelling, they had absorbed the rudiments of political literacy, and knew perfectly well what information about Matryona the State expected from them. The 'asesment' is not easy to read, but that probably didn't bother Sesov, and no one following the case after him could fail to be convinced by details which would freeze the heart of any loyal citizen. Matryona was deeply religious; she was not enthusiastic about collectivisation; her work lagged behind that of the more 'advanced' workers . . . And what the hell did it matter if the peasants could barely write? Sesov wasn't that well educated himself.

A procession of witnesses then appear before us – women farmworkers, village girls, women from Matryona's village, both of her own age and young enough to be her daughters. All of these women suffered the same female Russian fate as Matryona herself, and like Matryona few of them could read or sign the minutes of their interrogation. Yet each conversed with the State in a language of high political earnestness, eagerly judging Matryona in order to prove their own political orthodoxy.

Here is Matryona's relative, Maria Chuchalina ('cusin of the acused'):

'On July 13 1941, we were weeding milet on Chuchalilna's strip. During the rest break we discussed the war and then I think Matryona Chuchalina said lets get rid of sov. power then we can all pray to god again and then we could live like the old days, and the women started to tick her off. I heard them cursing her, but not what she said back, then I got up and said the state had helped her with her kids and even a five-year-old wouldn't say such a thing, and I told her it was the second time shed said it, and there were rumurs shed said it once at our club when I wasn't there . . .'

This weighty addition to Korevina's denunciation reveals yet another case of Matryona's 'counter-revolutionary agitation'. More follows.

Before the investigator the youngest witness appears, fourteen-year-old Masha Sarina, who has the clearest memory of what happened in the field:

'In Monakhov's field Anastasia read the newspaper and said the fasists want to stop soviet power, and Chuchalina said if there wasn't any soviet power the priests could come back and she could pray to God . . .'

Sixteen-year-old Katya Melnikova provided the investigator with an even more interesting picture. Young Katya was clearly spellbound by the solemnity of the occasion, and her own importance in unmasking Matryona's hostile secret self. Young Katya was clearly trying terribly hard . . .

'When they read the newspaper about the war with germany, Matryona Chuchalina said if our boys surenderd to the germans they would get the power and the priests could come back and then we could pray again and our life might get beter . . .'

Amongst all these statements, an anonymous red pencil has firmly underlined the words 'surenderd to the germans'. Matryona's crime has thus acquired the sinister dimensions of 'defeatist sentiments'.

Seven witnesses, not one of whom declined to take part in Matryona's persecution, let alone her defence. Not one 'I don't know', 'I didn't hear', 'I don't remember'. Seven witnesses who must have known full well that she hadn't a chance in hell against the machinations of the State.

What is the cause of this obsequiousness, which kills everything, all common sense, all sense of humour, and any compassion for

Matryona and her 'many children'? Investigator Sesov had no need to resort to torture, so thoroughly was the original denunciation pursued. Above all, it was the witnesses themselves, gazing at him with fear or devotion, who eagerly told him everything he wanted to hear from them. But since there was nothing to tell, and they weren't very adept at 'politics', they merely repeated over and over again variations on the theme of 'we'd be able to pray to God again . . .' and the young girls recalled the bit about 'surrendering to the Germans'.

Did they just imagine the whole thing in their terror at facing the people's investigator in the town of Stalinsk? It hardly matters whether they recalled it or invented it. What matters is what they said.

Immediately after interrogating the witnesses, Sesov ordered:

> Citizen Chuchalina is hereby charged that being disatisfied with Soviet power, she conducted counterevolutionary agitation amongst the farm-workers . . .

Who knows, within six months the 'plot' might be bubbling away amongst the enemies of the people! Sesov had no time to lose. Matryona must be 'held under armed guard at Kuznetsk prison No. 5'. From denunciation to prison took a mere twenty-four hours. Maybe even less. The exact times aren't recorded on the documents.

During her interrogation Matryona tried to defend herself. Sesov writes in her name:

> 'I am not guilty of the charges. I can prove that I conducted no ilegal agitaton, and if I did say something I dont remember it, i.e. my mind is not good since I was once struck by lightning and havent been able to think straight ever since. I don't know when or what I said, and I dont remember because my brain is confused.'

In other words, Matryona was acting the simpleton, as her one chance of freeing herself from the trap.

But you couldn't fool Sesov, Sesov was a lawyer! And he responded to Matryona's trick with a new order: psychiatric experts were appointed to the case and asked:

1 Is Citizen Chuchalina mentally ill?
2 Can she account for her actions, and take responsibility for them?

These 'expert investigations' were to be entrusted to Dr Yavorsky and forensic specialist Baranov. And once again a firm 'agreed' from prosecutor Shadrin.

The only person who didn't agree was Matryona the 'simpleton'. But by 19 July the doctors and experts had blown apart her defence.

> Examination of Citizen Chuchalina has revealed:
> No symptoms of any organic disorder of the nervous system.
> No psychological deviations from the norm, apart from a generally low level of cultural development.

Conclusion:

> Citizen Chuchalina is of sound mind and can account for her words and actions.

The mask of 'simpleton' was thus ruthlessly exposed. But for some reason Sesov also needed the conclusions of a gynaecologist. Perhaps they thought that forty-three-year-old Matryona might be pregnant. Not that this would have halted the Machine from its reprisals against the anti-Soviet menace . . . Yet inserted into the documents is a little slip of paper, informing all inquisitive participants in the persecution of Matryona that 'no pathological changes have been observed in the female sexual sphere', followed by a doctor's illegible signature.

We now know all about the Special Conferences 'without investigation or trial', which decided in an instant whether a person was to live or die, and if they were to live, exactly how and where. So we were somewhat surprised by all this show of legality in Matryona's case. Anxious about its reputation for propriety, the State wasn't scrimping on her investigation or trial. But if the inanity of her trial proves anything, it's how far from genuinely legal this State actually was.

After failing to convince anyone that she was a simpleton, Matryona changed tactics, and immediately after her examination, she told Sesov:

> '. . . I was weeding the milet in July 1941, and said to the girls after they'd read the paper, "lord grant us peace so we can all start praying again", but that about getting rid of soviet power and all living better without them, I know quite well I didn't say that to them. I have nothing to add to that.'

Matryona's 'level of cultural development' cannot have been so low if she was capable – in the interests of her own salvation – of thus rephrasing her own subversive utterances!

But it got her nowhere, and Sesov must have been well used to this sort of trick from 'enemies of the people'. Nothing could stop him now. On 21 July he wrote his 'Final Prosecution Evidence', in accordance with Article 58.

The universal 58 . . . What a simple way of destroying someone you know! Any idiot could do it, as long as they knew the address to send their denunciation to. Just seven days after Korevina's information Matryona was in prison, and her case had been transferred to the prosecutor at the Novosibirsk provincial court, a man named Shadrin.

The war raged on. Life behind the lines was in turmoil. Meanwhile Shadrin knew neither rest nor sleep and a military escort was standing by.

The minutes of Shadrin's interrogation of Matryona differ radically from the form which Sesov completed, for the prosecutor had to know much more about the accused than the investigator. He had to get her to answer nineteen questions, not merely on her social origins, but on her activities before and after the Revolution, whether she had served with any counter-revolutionary armies or joined any political parties, and so on.

Of course our Matryona had never belonged to any parties or armies, bound up as she was in her own female village life. Yet we learn much more about her from the prosecutor's questionnaire than from all the investigator's frantic scribblings.

> *Social origins* – poor peasantry.
> *Material situation of the accused or the accused's parents before the Revolution* – 2 cows, 2 horses, 5 sheep, 2 pigs.
> *Present material situation* – house, vegetable garden, 1 cow, 1 ox, 1 calf, 4 sheep, 12 hens.
> *How many dependent children and offspring of working age* – 5.

So Matryona had five children. The investigator had never bothered to find out what was meant by her 'many children'.

The prosecutor asked Matryona several other questions which the investigator in his slapdash way had never bothered with.

> QUESTION: Tell me, prisoner Chuchalina, wich of these witnesses here has it in for you, tell me there names?

ANSWER: The witnesses Monakhova, Melnikova and Sarina never did have it in for me but cusin Maria Chuchalina put them up to say I was a counter-revolutonary.
Q. How do you know that your cusin told the others to falsly say you were an agitater?
A. It is nown to me because the infestigator questoned me in our farm and I went home and said to Maria they probably done for me, what is it all about? Then Chuchalina answers yes we slanderd you and we all told him the same thing.

The prosecutor, evidently trying to get to the mundane roots of this 'state crime', gradually drags all Matryona's nasty family secrets out of her, and, despite his virtual illiteracy, he solemnly concludes that the plot was inspired by family quarrels to do with spiteful personalities, evil tongues, or the division of property. Yet even then, the 'slander' was qualified by a 'but'. He had asked who had it in for her, but without apparently understanding why, and once again he stubbornly ploughed on with his investigation:

Q. Tell me what the women in the milet-field said about the sov. Union's war with germany, who said it and what did they say?
A. The women read the paper about the war and what they said I dont remember, and after I said if the germans made peace we could all be able to pray again and life would be better and thats all I said . . .

After 120 minutes of interrogation they ended up exactly where they had started. Someone signed the minutes for Matryona, and Shadrin signed his name with a flourish.

On 25 September, the case was handed over to the prosecutor of Novosibirsk province. But that wasn't the end of the legal chicanery. Either Matryona's mundane seditious person required special attention from the State, or those in the regional office didn't trust Shadrin, but the deputy regional prosecutor, Nazaryuk, returned the case 'for further investigation', and suggested that Shadrin send Matryona to Tomsk mental hospital for psychiatric tests, 'since the results of the previous ones provide unconvincing evidence as to Chuchalina's mental competence'.

Matryona's fate, as she languished for the next three months in prison, was now controlled by the secret documents which made their slow progress through various offices. The letter authorising her transfer to Tomsk hospital reached Shadrin on 20 October. And a 'Report on forensic-psychiatric tests', signed by a group of Tomsk doctors, was dated 28 December.

This seems to have been the only literate document in the entire case. It is also a human document, which adds a new warmth and depth to Matryona's portrait:

> Hard-working life since childhood. Married at 18. 11 pregnancies, all resulting in live births. 7 surviving children. A calm, kind, trusting nature, and very religious . . . Well-adjusted, friendly and very sociable. Responds to questions eagerly and to the point. Lively conversationalist. Talks unwillingly about her case, attributing everything to religious conflicts.
>
> Behaves correctly. Works hard, disturbed by having to stay in hospital. Shows a great interest in her situation. Frequently asks the doctor: 'how will it all end?'
>
> Average intelligence. Relates critically to what is going on around her. Memory somewhat poor . . .

Now at last Matryona's fate rested in human hands. These intelligent, educated people, who understood everything and evidently liked her, would surely do everything in their power to save her from the ravages of Article 58. As professionals, they could surely pull it off, and write – in the name of mercy, and Matryona's seven children (seven! why did Shadrin write five?) – that despite all her sociability she had lost her wits. Surely they could describe her as mentally ill, and release the Machine from the need to punish her for her heinous crime.

Whether deliberately or not, Nazaryuk had given the doctors the chance to intervene with the State in Matryona's case, and to put a stop to the whole thing with a simple diagnosis. Not 'repressive psychiatry', such as we're always unfortunately hearing about now, but 'charitable psychiatry', defending one little tree in a forest which is being destroyed.

Alas, whether because they didn't understand, or lacked the courage, or were too zealous, the five doctors at the Tomsk psychiatric hospital, including the chief consultant and a professor, categorically concluded their portrait:

> There is no sign of mental disturbance, therefore she must be regarded as responsible for the act of which she is accused.

On 9 March, Shadrin conducted yet another interrogation. And yet again we hear the same words: 'I didn't say that about getting rid of Soviet power.'

The minutes of that interrogation do at least reveal how many children Matryona has, however, and why Shadrin had written 'five dependents'. 'Seven offspring,' we now read, 'aged between three and twenty-three, two of them serving in the Soviet Army.'

Perhaps these two soldiers were fighting somewhere far from their native village to defend Leningrad or Moscow, the Black Sea or the Baltic. And while they were defending their country, their mother was in prison, being subjected in the name of her country to endless, interminable questioning . . .

There are twenty-five more pages of this ludicrous and terrible case, each question more stupid than the last.

> Q. You told the investigator during the interogation of 17.VII.41 that you had a bad memory due to the fact that 7 years ago you were struck by lightning and so canot remember what you said to the women at the milet field on 8.VII.41 and 12–14.
> A. I told the investigator that my memory is weak, i.e. my mind isn't good, maybe I did say it.
> Q. Then tell me why at the interrogation of 9.11.42 you told me that on 17.VII.41 you hadnt told the investigator that your memory was bad and that you werent in your right mind . . .

As we read on, it seems increasingly clear that Shadrin is the one who is mad.

The third version of the charge (identical to the first and second versions), signed by Shadrin, finally put special prosecutor Nazaryuk in charge of the case, for some reason. On 6 April, Nazaryuk sent the case to the president of the Novosibirsk provincial court, where lawyers decided quickly and impartially to 'hear the case *in camera* before a prosecutor and barrister'.

'A barrister'! Ah yes, we had a 'legal state' then. But whom did it serve, and who had the right to avail themselves of it? Matryona had the right to be condemned by the Sesovs, Shadrins, and Nazaryuks of this world. A living person had the right to be tortured on the rack of the infernal Machine. Denunciation had the right to cut short someone's life, so that the Machine was soon fuelled by endless denunciations.

The case was heard on 18 April 1942 in Stalinsk, thirty miles from the Novostroika collective farm. With almost all the men away at the front, it was the women who farmed, worked in the factories, and became judges. The fact that the three on this case were all women makes the State's concern for the Sesovs and Shadrins even harder to understand. Why had they been saved from the front? So that they could do battle with Matryona in the rear? You must be important, Matryona. All because of you, the State has spared these men from the rifle and settled them in nice comfortable office jobs . . .

They needed rifles to guard a dangerous criminal like Matryona, though. 'The accused appeared in court under armed guard,' we read.

But the trial didn't start on 18 April, for although the witnesses were 'summoned by the prosecutor of the Kuznetsk district', they failed to appear, for 'reasons unknown'.

Matryona had now spent nine months in prison. Her children were abandoned, her husband was hitting the bottle. Perhaps the witnesses imagined themselves in Matryona's place and were horrified by what they had done, their faith in official justice shattered. But this is no place for the imagination . . .

The trial was postponed to 22 June 1942. And Matryona was once again escorted into the courtroom under armed guard. 'The witnesses Ivanova, Chuchalina, Melnikova, Sarina and Monakhova appear,' we read. Then the same old gramophone record starts up: 'She said if only we could get rid of soviet power . . .'

Prosecutor Plakhov considers the charges against Matryona to be fully proved, and 'asks for a long sentence'. Barrister Glossberg timidly asks for leniency, 'in view of her illiteracy and her many children, and the fact that she has two sons in the army'. And Matryona herself finally begs for a lenient sentence, 'on account of having two sons defending their Country'.

What did these women feel when they saw Matryona under armed guard, after almost a year in prison? Or were they too brought to court under armed guard?

How should we regard them now? With contempt or with pity? Should we shudder in revulsion at such cringing servility, capable of violating everything human in the name of . . . What? Under what pressures? In what ignorance and agony?

We know nothing of their agony, or what they felt as they stood listening to the SENTENCE:

Citizen Chuchalina to be subjected to six years' loss of liberty
in corrective labour camps, without loss of property. Plus an
additional three years' loss of rights.

We do not know how they were greeted in the village on their
return, or how they managed to face Matryona's motherless children, or what happened when she returned, or whether they even
survived to see it.

We know only that Novostroika called them as witnesses of
Matryona's crime, revealed to the State by a denunciation, and that
they played their full part in this cruel theatre of the absurd, even
though none of them had ever learned to read or write.

The women judges were probably congratulating themselves.
They could have given Matryona ten years, after all, yet they ordered
her to rot in captivity for a mere six. They didn't even take away her
hens, or her children. Yes indeed, a humane sentence.

The only witness not to appear was twenty-seven-year-old Anna
Ponomareva, who 'disappeared, it is not known where'. Perhaps
Ponomareva's soul had driven her far from her native village, where
the ghost of Matryona would give her no rest. But such idle specu-
lations are feeble indeed compared to the unimaginable power of
Denunciation!

All the archival documents of the cases we have read were instigated
by denunciations.

Our society now bears an enormous responsibility for these archives. As we now attempt to reorganise ourselves, thousands of such
files must be opened up. Not so as to punish the informers. They
lived at a time when denunciation was judged not as a foul and filthy
deed, but as the proper way for a loyal citizen to behave. Not all were
informers, but there were many who were.

Without informers, the Machine of repression might have quietly
rusted away from disuse somewhere in the remote depths of the
empire. Instead it rolled on, swallowing up ploughmen and poets,
gardeners and blacksmiths – like the unknown Mitrofan Artamonov,
who was the same age as Matryona and received ten years in
corrective labour camps, without confiscation of property, 'because
of the non-existence of such', but with an additional five years' loss of
rights, 'in accordance with Art. 31 a. and b. of the Criminal Code'.
All because he complained during a smoking break that 'it's a lot of

rubish caling Stalin clever – you should look at Rykov, now, he's got brains!'

And so the Machine rolled on, thanks to the inexhaustible passion for denunciation, a passion which to this day turns many a brave soul to ashes.

We must read the records, not to hang messages over people's graves reading 'Informer', 'Hangman', or 'Persecutor'. We, the living, need this information so that we may at last understand our own tragic complicity in the senseless victimisation of Matryona and Mitrofan, the peasant and the blacksmith, successors to those same Workers and Peasants in the sculpture, who symbolise the triumph of the new Soviet system. We must know about them, and so must our children, and our grandchildren. We must know, and suffer, and create a Public Committee of Protection from the evil of Stalinism – a Memorial of Conscience.

The Memorial Movement must gather together all the grey files rotting away in all the archives of the country, and say to people: go and look at yourselves! Read these illiterate denunciations, these insane plots, these foolish justifications, these 'humane' sentences! Experience your last night before being shot. Set off for a camp. Rehabilitate yourself and nearly die in the process. Tremble, cry, fear, and destroy yourself, so that you end up hating yourself. And finally understand that only those incapable of denunciation and betrayal, in whoever's name, can save you from the totalitarian state.

Forgive us, Matryona. Forgive us ordinary people for pushing you into the steel jaw of the Machine, where you probably didn't even manage to pray to God for your crime.

Forgive us – we are better now. You never did 'get rid of the soviet state', and nowadays your priests appear on television and have meetings with our leaders.

Forgive us, Matryona. We'll do everything to make a country for our children and your grandchildren which has no place for informers . . .

So how should it look, this monument to the victims of denunciation?

Photograph Acknowledgements

Vitaly Korotich by Gianni Giansanti/SYGMA, *Telegraph* Weekend Magazine, 30 September 1989

The rest of the photographs come from *Ogonyok* in the following order:

Issue	Date	Page	Photographer
No. 39,	1988,	p. 28	V. Zhuk
No. 39,	1988,	p. 29	Y. Oreshkin (Special photographer of the Ministry of Interior Affairs)
No. 27,	1988,	p. 13	V. Debabov
No. 51,	1988,	p. 28	L. Sherstennikov
No. 51,	1988,	p. 27	L. Sherstennikov
No. 14,	1988,	p. 16	V. Bazhyonov and V. Peterburzhskogo
No. 51,	1988,	p. 1	I. Gavrilov
No. 51,	1988,	p. 2	I. Gavrilov
No. 12,	1989,	p. 21	Y. Rost
No. 51,	1988,	p. 3	I. Gavrilov
No. 51,	1988,	p. 3	I. Gavrilov
No. 43,	1988,	p. 3	A. Treplyov
No. 30,	1988,	p. 15	V. Shchekoldin
No. 38,	1988,	p. 15	M. Steinbok
No. 32,	1988,	p. 14	A. Lukyanov
No. 14,	1988,	p. 12	P. Krivtsov
No. 35,	1989,	p. 1	I. Gavrilov
No. 32,	1988,	p. 16	I. Gavrilov
No. 32,	1988,	p. 18	I. Gavrilov
No. 32,	1988,	p. 19	I. Gavrilov
No. 22,	1989,	p. 11	D. Grafov

No. 12,   1989,   p. 32   M. Steinbok
No. 39,   1988,   p. 22   E. Aksyonov and E. Ettinger
No. 42,   1988,   p. 21   S. Petrukhin
No. 49,   1988,   p. 32   D. Baltermants and D. Debabov
No. 9,   1989,   p. 14   A. Mitta
No. 27,   1988,   p. 12   V. Debabov
No. 17,   1989,   p. 21   B. Davydov